ALL ABOUT SILK

A FABRIC DICTIONARY & SWATCHBOOK

WRITTEN & ILLUSTRATED BY JULIE PARKER

Copyright© 1991 by Julie Parker.
Revised edition copyright 1992.
Sixth printing 2000.

Published by Rain City Publishing
Seattle, Washington

Book design, cover design, text and all illustrations by Julie Parker.

Fabric Reference Series, Volume I

Address inquiries to:
Rain City Publishing
P.O. Box 15378
Seattle, WA 98115-0378
Phone: 206-527-8778
Fax: 206-526-2871
E-mail: RainCityPu@aol.com
Web site: www.raincitypublishing.com

Printed in the United States of America.

**Library of Congress
Cataloging-in-Publication Data**
Parker, Julie
    All about silk: a fabric dictionary
& swatchbook/text & illustrations by
Julie Parker.
        p.   cm.
Fabric reference series; v. 1.
    Includes bibliographical references
        (p. 89) and index.
    ISBN 0-9637612-0-X
    1. Silk fabrics – Silk. I. Title. II.
Series.
TS1665.P37 1991
677/.39 20   93117999//r93

CONTENTS

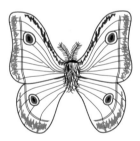

TYPES OF SILK

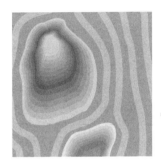

THE WORLD OF SILK

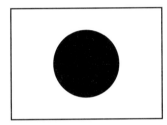

CARE OF SILK

SILK CHARACTERISTICS

THE WEAVES

TYPES OF YARN

SPECIAL EFFECTS

MISCELLANEOUS NOTES

THE
WORLD
OF SILK

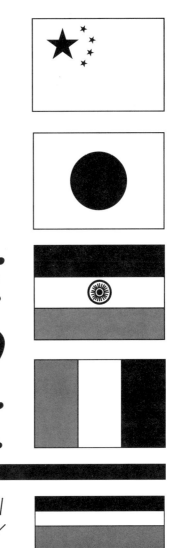

INTRODUCTION
HISTORY & INDUSTRY
THE SILK MOTH

INTRODUCTION

I wrote this book because I wanted to know what I was looking at when I went to the fabric store. I have been sewing for more than 20 years, but until recently, fabric made no more sense to me than it did when I made my first dress back in the sixth grade.

A trip to the fabric store was inspiring and confusing. Colors and textures caught my eye, but I knew little about the different types of fabrics and their characteristics.

I was familiar with terms like twill, tissue faille and crepe, but I didn't know what they meant. I didn't understand the distinction between crepe chiffon and chiffon taffeta. I thought organdy and organza were the same thing. I thought damask and jacquard were different.

When I began to ask questions, I didn't get satisfactory answers. I got more confused. And I discovered that many other people who work with fabric don't know any more about it than I did.

I consulted sewing and textile books, and quickly discovered that some fabrics have three or four names, some terms describe three or four fabrics, and some terms have three or four spellings. It's normal to be confused.

The language of textiles

I was overwhelmed by vague and conflicting descriptions and industry jargon. Textile dictionaries are quite technical: They speak of picks and ends, bilateral fibers, warp beams, eight-harness looms, weft yarns, calendering, gassing, singeing and face-finished goods.

None of that makes much sense to me. What I want to know is how each fabric looks, feels and behaves, how to use it and how to care for it. I want to know how much I can expect to pay for it and where to buy it. When I pay $30 a yard for three yards of silk, I want to make that purchase with confidence in my ability to choose the right fabric for my project.

Those who lack confidence in their fabric-selecting skills are advised to stick to the list of fabrics suggested on the back of most pattern envelopes. This is not as easy as it sounds, for two reasons:

■ The lists usually include confusing, oversimplified or vague terminology.

■ Even when the information is clear, it is not very useful, because fabric stores seldom use such terms to label their products.

Most fabric labels include the fiber content, the price and, in many cases, a recommended method of care. Some stores routinely provide additional information about the weave, the country of origin, the

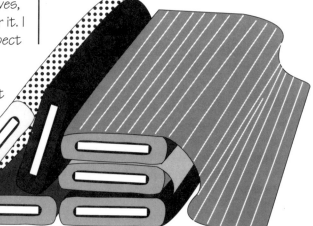

fabric's weight and so forth, while others make no effort to do so.

This is not a conspiracy to keep customers in the dark. Many stores do not identify fabric types because they simply don't know what they are.

For starters, only a few fabric types can be easily identified and accurately labeled. Descriptions of similar types of fabrics often overlap; distinctions are not clear and usually represent someone's preference or opinion rather than fact. You might call a fabric "damask," while I prefer to call it "jacquard." We would both be right.

There aren't any rules

That's because there are no hard and fast rules about defining fabric. The textile industry is creative and competitive, driven by consumer demands for fashion and function. Weaves, fibers, dyes and finishes can be mixed together in a mind-boggling number of combinations. As fabrics evolve, definitions change.

Adding to the confusion is the natural desire of textile mills and garment manufacturers to market their products by suggesting an air of distinction, novelty or exclusivity.

> **"When I pay $30 a yard for three yards of silk, I want to make that purchase with confidence in my ability to choose the right fabric. "**

The easiest way to do this is to give the product a catchy name. And almost anything goes, as long as the manufacturer gives equal time to the fabric's fiber content.

The catchy name may refer to the fiber, the weave, the finish or the garment itself, resulting in a jumble of confusing terms. A number of very different items often wind up bearing similar names, even when they have nothing in common.

The confusion is compounded when an item becomes popular enough to receive media attention. Constant use of a catchy marketing term often creates the impression that the name refers to a standard type of fabric with clearly defined characteristics, when it does not.

Finally, some fabrics don't have assigned names. Mills frequently use

numbers, rather than names, because it is easier to keep track of fabric No. 3754 than "lightweight silk crepe with jacquard figures." When one of these numbered fabrics is described in terms of fabric types, it is based on the expertise and opinion of the person giving the description, rather than an industry standard for the fabric.

Novelty vs. staple fabrics

In spite of this, some fabrics are easily defined. It's not difficult at all to conjure up an image of corduroy, velvet, denim or canvas. Most people can visualize a terry cloth bathrobe and an oxford shirt.

These are what the textile industry calls staple fabrics. Staple fabrics have steady sales over an extended period of time. They are produced in response to a large and continuous demand, they have been around for years and they aren't going to disappear in the near future.

Novelty fabrics are variations of staple fabrics. They usually resemble certain fabrics, even if they aren't exactly the same. So while it is next to impossible to accurately define all fabrics, it is easy to describe staple fabrics and to apply that knowledge to everything else. That's where this book fits in.

How to use this book

This book is about silk, although many of the fabrics featured here are made from other fibers as well. Most of the fabrics are fairly common and usually available in several weights and various incarnations.

The 32 fabrics are organized in alphabetical order, but you do not need to start at the beginning. The book's design invites you to jump in anywhere and skip around.

Two pages are devoted to each fabric. On the left-hand page, you will find a detailed description of the fabric and how it is made (1), a small sample of a typical version of the fabric (2) and a mini-vocabulary (3) of similar fabrics, related items or terms that need more explanation.

On the other page, a checklist highlights the fabric's main sewing characteristics, its price, suggested styles and methods of care.

The boxes on both pages (4, 5) are filled with descriptions of yarns, weaves, finishes and special effects, bits of history and other tidbits.

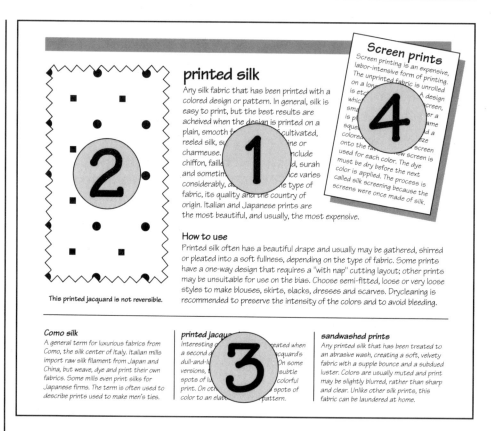

This printed jacquard is not reversible.

printed silk
Any silk fabric that has been printed with a colored design or pattern. In general, silk is easy to print, but the best results are acheived when the design is printed on a plain, smooth f........ cultivated, reeled silk, s........ ine or charmeuse. .... nclude chiffon, faill............ d, surah and sometim............ ce varies considerably, d............ e type of fabric, its quality and the country of origin. Italian and Japanese prints are the most beautiful, and usually, the most expensive.

Screen prints
Screen printing is an expensive, labor-intensive form of printing. The unprinted fabric is unrolled on a lon............ A design is etc............ which .... screen, sma............ ame is p............ d a sque............ eze colored............ onto the fa............ ew screen is used for each color. The dye must be dry before the next color is applied. The process is called silk screening because the screens were once made of silk.

How to use
Printed silk often has a beautiful drape and usually may be gathered, shirred or pleated into a soft fullness, depending on the type of fabric. Some prints have a one-way design that requires a "with nap" cutting layout; other prints may be unsuitable for use on the bias. Choose semi-fitted, loose or very loose styles to make blouses, skirts, slacks, dresses and scarves. Drycleaning is recommended to preserve the intensity of the colors and to avoid bleeding.

Como silk
A general term for luxurious fabrics from Como, the silk center of Italy. Italian mills import raw silk filament from Japan and China, but weave, dye and print their own fabrics. Some mills even print silks for Japanese firms. The term is often used to describe prints used to make men's ties.

printed jacqua...
Interesting .... reated when a second d............ acquard's dull-and-li............ On some versions, ... subtle spots of lu............ colorful print. On ot............ spots of color to an elab............ pattern.

sandwashed prints
Any printed silk that has been treated to an abrasive wash, creating a soft, velvety fabric with a supple bounce and a subdued luster. Colors are usually muted and print may be slightly blurred, rather than sharp and clear. Unlike other silk prints, this fabric can be laundered at home.

The checklist
The checklist gives at-a-glance details on the following subjects:
■ A. Sewing rating
This refers to the degree of difficulty involved in working with the fabric. Beginners, for example, would be wise to avoid fabrics that are difficult to cut and sew.

■ B. Suggested fit
This refers to terms used by pattern companies to describe the fitting and design ease built into each garment. The information can be found on the back of the pattern envelope. A chart in the back of the pattern book gives more precise dimensions for each level of ease.

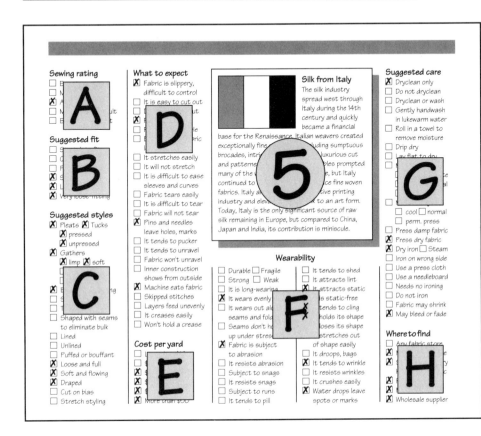

Sewing rating
- [ ] E...
- [ ] M...
- [X] A...
- [ ] M... ...lt
- [ ] E... t

Suggested fit
- [ ] e
- [ ] F
- [X]
- [X] L
- [X] Very loose fitting

Suggested styles
- [X] Pleats [X] Tucks
- [X] pressed
- [X] unpressed
- [X] Gathers
- [X] limp [X] soft
- [X] ...
- [ ] S...
- [ ] T...
- [ ] Shaped with seams to eliminate bulk
- [ ] Lined
- [ ] Unlined
- [ ] Puffed or bouffant
- [X] Loose and full
- [X] Soft and flowing
- [X] Draped
- [ ] Cut on bias
- [ ] Stretch styling

What to expect
- [X] Fabric is slippery, difficult to control
- [ ] It is easy to cut out
- [ ] ...cut
- [X]
- [ ] ...le
- [ ] ...ric
- [ ] It stretches easily
- [ ] It will not stretch
- [ ] It is difficult to ease sleeves and curves
- [ ] Fabric tears easily
- [ ] It is difficult to tear
- [ ] Fabric will not tear
- [X] Pins and needles leave holes, marks
- [ ] It tends to pucker
- [ ] It tends to unravel
- [ ] Fabric won't unravel
- [ ] Inner construction shows from outside
- [X] Machine eats fabric
- [ ] Skipped stitches
- [ ] Layers feed unevenly
- [ ] It creases easily
- [ ] Won't hold a crease

Cost per yard
- [ ]
- [X] $
- [X] $
- [X] $
- [X] $
- [X] More than $00

Silk from Italy
The silk industry spread west through Italy during the 14th century and quickly became a financial base for the Renaissance. Italian weavers created exceptionally fine ... ...luding sumptuous brocades, intri... ...luxurious cut and patterne... ...les prompted many of the ... ..., but Italy continued to ... ...ce fine woven fabrics. Italy a... ...tive printing industry and elev... ...to an art form. Today, Italy is the only significant source of raw silk remaining in Europe, but compared to China, Japan and India, its contribution is miniscule.

Wearability
- [ ] Durable [ ] Fragile
- [ ] Strong [ ] Weak
- [ ] It is long-wearing
- [X] It wears evenly
- [ ] It wears out al...
- [ ] seams and fold...
- [ ] Seams don't h... up under stres...
- [X] Fabric is subject to abrasion
- [ ] It resists abrasion
- [ ] Subject to snags
- [ ] It resists snags
- [ ] Subject to runs
- [ ] It tends to pill

- [ ] It tends to shed
- [ ] It attracts lint
- [X] It attracts static
- [ ] ...s static-free
- [ ] ...tends to cling
- [ ] ...holds its shape
- [ ] ...oses its shape
- [ ] ...stretches out of shape easily
- [ ] It droops, bags
- [X] It tends to wrinkle
- [ ] It resists wrinkles
- [ ] It crushes easily
- [X] Water drops leave spots or marks

Suggested care
- [X] Dryclean only
- [ ] Do not dryclean
- [ ] Dryclean or wash
- [ ] Gently handwash in lukewarm water
- [ ] Roll in a towel to remove moisture
- [ ] Drip dry
- [ ] Lay flat to dry
- [ ]
- [ ] cool [ ] normal
- [ ] perm. press
- [ ] Press damp fabric
- [X] Press dry fabric
- [X] Dry iron [ ] Steam
- [ ] Iron on wrong side
- [ ] Use a press cloth
- [ ] Use a needleboard
- [ ] Needs no ironing
- [ ] Do not iron
- [ ] Fabric may shrink
- [X] May bleed or fade

Where to find
- [ ] Any fabric store
- [X]
- [X]
- [X]
- [X] Wholesale supplier

Vogue, for example, adds 3-4 inches of ease to a semi-fitted blouse and more than 8 inches to a very loose-fitting blouse. Each company uses a different formula.

■ C. Suggested styles

This refers to a garment's shape and appearance, rather than its fit. The most successful garments are made from fabric that is compatible with the style. For example, fabric that won't hold a crease probably isn't the best choice for pleats.

■ D. What to expect

This refers to characteristics that affect the construction phase. For example, a tight weave may be difficult to ease, especially around sleeves and curved seams, while a very sheer fabric may require special treatment of facings and seams.

■ E. Cost per yard

This refers to the retail price, which usually reflects quality and the cost of labor. Shop around – prices vary from one store to another.

■ F. Wearability

This section describes how the fabric behaves as a garment. Does the fabric wear evenly? Does it tend to pill, cling or wrinkle easily?

■ G. Suggested care

Silk fiber is washable, but many silk fabrics should be drycleaned. The weave, dye, finish and garment style all affect the method of care.

■ H. Where to find

Some stores don't carry silk. Others carry some, but not all, of the fabrics in this book. Some fabrics are seasonal. Mail-order sources advertise in sewing magazines.

One final note

Keep in mind that every version of every fabric differs a little or a lot from other versions of the same fabric. This book does not have all the answers – it merely explains what you might expect to find.

S ILK HISTORY AND INDUSTRY

Silk cultivation is called sericulture, from the Latin *sericum*, which means cultivation of silk. The Chinese were the first to develop silk and reel it from the cocoon, starting in about 2640 B.C. The most common legend credits silk discovery to a Chinese empress, who accidentally dropped a cocoon into hot water, causing it to unravel. For almost 3,000 years, China maintained a monopoly on the luxurious fiber, but their carefully guarded secret eventually leaked to Japan and India.

Silk cultivation was introduced to the West in about 552 A.D., when two monks smuggled silkworms into Constantinople. From there, the silk industry spread to Italy, Spain and throughout Europe, providing a financial base for the Renaissance from about 1400 to the mid 1800s.

The British were not successful at breeding silkworms, so they tried to establish sericulture in the American colonies. By 1838, the American silk industry appeared to have a bright future, but the venture collapsed a year later. The industry declined in Europe as well, and today, the main sources of silk are the original three: China, Japan and India.

This lack of success by other countries is not surprising. Silk cultivation is a difficult process, one that requires the right environment and a great deal of time and effort.

The process begins with the silk moth, which lays hundreds of tiny eggs about the size of a pinhead. The eggs are carefully examined and diseased eggs arc discarded. The remaining eggs are divided into two groups, one for reproduction and one for production of cocoons. Once they pass inspection, the eggs are put into cold storage for six to 10 months until the mulberry trees begin to bud.

The silkworm

After a brief incubation period, the eggs hatch into larvae. For the next 20 to 30 days, the larvae live in a carefully

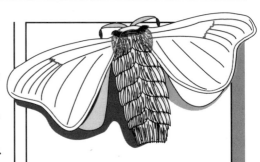

THE SILK MOTH

The *Bombyx mori* is the most common and prolific domesticated silk moth. It was originally found in China, but is now bred in all of the silk-producing countries and is no longer found in its native habitat.

Its caterpillar, commonly called a silkworm, eats mulberry leaves and spins a small, reelable cocoon of fine white or yellow silk that is regular and consistent. There are several other species of Bombyx moths as well as new varieties developed by breeders. Some produce only one cocoon a year (monovoltine), while others produce two or more (polyvoltine).

All species of the Bombyx genus eat mulberry leaves and produce reelable cocoons. Other silk moths eat juniper, oak and fig leaves, and produce different types of cocoons, some of which cannot be reeled. The *Bombyx mori* is also called *Bombyx fortunatus* and *Bombyx textor*.

controlled environment and eat a special diet of cleaned, chopped mulberry leaves. During this time, they grow rapidly, shed their skins four times, and mature into grayish-white caterpillars about 3 to 4 inches long, called silkworms.

The little buggers are ravenous, but quite picky: The mulberry leaves must be clean, dry and the same age as themselves. If conditions are less than perfect, the silkworm will produce inferior silk or no silk at all.

When the silkworm has finished growing, it stops eating and begins to spin a cocoon to protect it during the final stage of the cycle — transformation into a moth.

The silk cocoon

The silkworms are placed on wooden racks that are sectioned with cardboard and stacked about 10 high — sort of a high-rise apartment for caterpillars. Each silkworm has its own compartment to spin its cocoon, which helps to keep the cocoons from getting tangled.

The cocoon is really an oval shell or casing about an inch long. The silkworm extrudes a syrupy fluid from two silk glands in its head. The fluid instantly hardens into two silk filaments, called brin, which are held together by a sticky substance, called sericin, secreted from another set of glands. The double filament forms a single strand, called bave.

The silkworm moves its head from side to side in a figure-eight motion, crossing the strand to build layer after layer of the cocoon from the outside in. It spins continuously for 24 to 72 hours, shrinking in size as it goes, until the cocoon is done.

If nature were allowed to take its course, a soft, fuzzy, cream-colored moth would break out of the cocoon in about 12 days by emitting a liquid to dissolve a hole in the silk.

Unfortunately for the new moth, silk is more valuable when the long filament is not broken. The finished cocoon is baked, steamed, gassed or refrigerated to stifle the moth and prevent it from damaging the silk.

A single, unbroken cocoon yields from 1,600 feet to more than a mile of continuous filament, in contrast to the short fibers of cotton, wool, linen and other natural fibers. The

SILK'S ALLURE

Silk is an almost mystical fiber, sought after and fought over for centuries. Here are some of the qualities that make it so desirable:

▲ **Luster**
The smooth silk fiber reflects light, creating a luster and beauty unmatched by other natural fibers.

▲ **Strength**
Silk is the strongest natural fiber for its weight. Nylon is the only synthetic fiber that is as strong.

▲ **Color**
Silk is easy to dye, so fabrics are often brightly colored or iridescent. Prints take so well that the back looks almost as good as the front.

▲ **Durability**
Silk is tougher than cotton and fine wool, but not as durable as linen or coarse wool. It resists molds and mildews that cause fibers to rot.

▲ **Elasticity**
Silk will stretch up to 20 percent without breaking. It is also resilient, meaning it springs back into shape.

▲ **It breathes**
Silk is porous, which allows the skin to breathe. The absorbent fiber wicks moisture away from the body.

▲ **Warmth**
Silk provides warmth without the weight or itch of wool.

length of silk makes it possible to produce fabrics unlike anything else (although some of today's synthetic fibers come close).

Reeled silk

Other natural fibers are cleaned, carded, combed and spun. Silk is reeled. This is done by soaking the cocoons in hot water to soften the sericin and loosen the silk. The surface of each cocoon is lightly brushed to find the end of the filament. Several of these exceedingly fine strands are collected and reeled into a single, untwisted thread, held together by the sericin. Two to 10 cocoons may be used to form this single strand of reeled, raw silk.

The next step is called "throwing," from the Anglo-Saxon word thraw, meaning to twist or spin. A throwster sorts the skeins of raw silk for quality. Then the reeled silk is grouped and twisted into different types of thread, commonly called yarns, used to weave fabric. Two or more strands of reeled silk are used to form the different silk yarns.

Finally, the silk is degummed of part or all of its sericin, usually by boiling the yarn or fabric in a soapy solution. The more sericin boiled off, the better quality the silk. When the silk is degummed, it becomes much softer, more lustrous and generally more desirable.

Once it has been degummed, the whitened silk can be dyed or printed. Cultivated silk dyes especially well, so fabrics are often brightly colored.

Other uses

The use of silk is not limited to the textile industry. It can be found in a wide variety of other products, including face powder, cold cream, wigs, dental floss and braces, bicycle tires, tennis-racket strings, fishing lines, parachutes, hot-air balloons, surgical sutures and bandages, electrical insulation and crosshairs in optical instruments.

Benjamin Franklin used a silk kite to conduct his famous experiments and silk fabric is used in the nose of the supersonic jet, the Concorde.

In some parts of the world, the cocoon's stifled, undeveloped moth is considered a treat to eat.

SILK'S LIMITATIONS

Silk is regarded by some as nature's most perfect fiber. But even perfection has its limitations:

▼ **Soap and agitation**
Silk's smooth surface does not attract dirt and is easily cleaned. But silk can be damaged by most laundry detergents – always use a mild soap. Silk loses strength when wet, so do not wring or agitate.

▼ **Bleach**
Silk is easily damaged by strong bleaches that contain sodium hypochlorite. Mild bleach of sodium perborate or hydrogen peroxide is allowable, but use caution.

▼ **Heat and light**
Silk is sensitive to heat and begins to decompose at 330° Fahrenheit. Use a warm, rather than hot, iron. Drapery and upholstery fabrics should be protected from direct exposure to light, which weakens silk faster than cotton or wool.

▼ **Mildew and moths**
Silk will not mildew except in extreme conditions. Moths don't care for it, but carpet beetles prefer silk.

▼ **Perspiration**
Perspiration causes silk to deteriorate and affects the color, causing staining. Any silk worn next to the skin should be cleaned frequently.

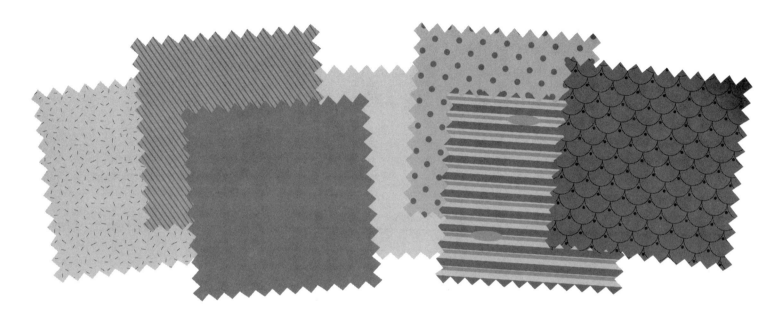

32 SILK FABRICS

DEFINITIONS & SWATCHES

ATTACH SAMPLE HERE

LENGTHWISE GRAIN

Batiste de soie is smooth and lustrous.

batiste de soie

French for "silk batiste." A fine, lightweight fabric made with a tight plain weave and very fine, tightly twisted yarns. Fabric is sheer, with a delicate, limp, soft hand and a smooth, lustrous surface that resists snagging. It is similar in weight and hand to China silk, but authentic batiste is more tightly woven, more lustrous and of better quality. China silk is available in a wide range of colors; silk batiste is usually bleached white or dyed pastel shades. It may be plain or figured.

How to use

Batiste de soie has a gentle drape that falls into soft flares. It may be shirred or gathered into a limp fullness. Seams, facings and hems can be seen from the finished side of the garment. The fabric is stable and strong, but requires gentle handling and a very fine, sharp needle. Choose fitted, semi-fitted or loose-fitting styles to make blouses and lightweight summer dresses. Fabric may be drycleaned or gently washed by hand. Squeeze in a towel and drip dry. Iron garment while fabric is slightly damp.

Batiste fabrics

The first batiste was a fine, soft, sheer, lightweight linen made with a plain weave. It was developed by and named for Jean Baptiste, a 13th century French linen weaver. Today, the fabric is usually made of pure cotton or a blend of cotton and polyester. It is used to make fine, lightweight blouses and summer dresses, expensive baby clothes and embroidered handkerchiefs, nightgowns and lingerie. Variations made from linen, wool and rayon are usually used for blouses and dresses.

---

lawn

A very fine, somewhat sheer, tightly woven cotton fabric made with a plain weave and fine, combed single yarns. It is sometimes called batiste or nainsook, but authentic lawn is slightly heavier and has more body. The finest lawns are made by Liberty of London, known for its exquisite prints.

mull

A soft, thin, plain-weave fabric made with very fine yarns of cotton, silk or a blend of the two. Like batiste, it is usually bleached or dyed pastel colors. It is also called China mull, India mull or French mull, especially when made of silk. Swiss mull is sized. Mull is not very common in the United States.

silk muslin

A very thin silk fabric made with a loose, open weave in solid colors, woven raised figures or small multicolored patterns.

Swiss batiste

A very fine batiste made from long-staple cotton and treated with a lustrous finish.

Sewing rating
- [ ] Easy to sew
- [x] Moderately easy
- [ ] Average
- [ ] Moderately difficult
- [ ] Extremely difficult

Suggested fit
- [ ] Stretch to fit
- [ ] Close-fitting
- [x] Fitted
- [x] Semi-fitted
- [x] Loose-fitting
- [ ] Very loose-fitting

Suggested styles
- [x] Pleats [x] Tucks
  - [x] pressed
  - [ ] unpressed
- [x] Gathers
  - [x] limp [x] soft
  - [ ] full [ ] lofty
  - [ ] bouffant
- [x] Elasticized shirring
- [ ] Smocked
- [x] Tailored
- [ ] Shaped with seams to eliminate bulk
- [ ] Lined
- [ ] Unlined
- [ ] Puffed or bouffant
- [ ] Loose and full
- [x] Soft and flowing
- [x] Draped
- [ ] Cut on bias
- [ ] Stretch styling

What to expect
- [x] Fabric is slippery, difficult to control
- [ ] It is easy to cut out
- [ ] Difficult to cut out
- [ ] Fabric has a nap
- [x] Fabric is reversible
- [x] Both sides of fabric look the same
- [ ] It stretches easily
- [ ] It will not stretch
- [x] It is difficult to ease sleeves and curves
- [x] Fabric tears easily
- [ ] It is difficult to tear
- [ ] Fabric will not tear
- [x] Pins and needles leave holes, marks
- [ ] It tends to pucker
- [ ] It tends to unravel
- [ ] Fabric won't unravel
- [x] Inner construction shows from outside
- [x] Machine eats fabric
- [ ] Skipped stitches
- [ ] Layers feed unevenly
- [x] It creases easily
- [ ] Won't hold a crease

Cost per yard
- [ ] Less than $10
- [x] $10 to $20
- [ ] $20 to $30
- [ ] $30 to $40
- [ ] $40 to $50
- [ ] More than $50

The plain weave
Most fabrics are woven from one of the three basic weaves — plain, twill and satin. The plain weave is the simplest and most common of the three. Every lengthwise (warp) yarn passes over-under-over-under every crosswise (filling) yarn, forming a checkerboard pattern. Fabrics print beautifully and wear evenly, but they wrinkle badly, tear easily and tend to shrink. They are not as strong or firm as twill and do not drape as well. Twill and satin fabrics are more absorbent. Plain-weave silks include crepe, chiffon, China silk, georgette, organza and taffeta.

Wearability
- [x] Durable [ ] Fragile
- [ ] Strong [ ] Weak
- [x] It is long-wearing
- [x] It wears evenly
- [ ] It wears out along seams and folds
- [ ] Seams don't hold up under stress
- [ ] Fabric is subject to abrasion
- [ ] It resists abrasion
- [ ] Subject to snags
- [x] It resists snags
- [ ] Subject to runs
- [ ] It tends to pill
- [ ] It tends to shed
- [ ] It attracts lint
- [x] It attracts static
- [ ] It is static-free
- [ ] It tends to cling
- [x] It holds its shape
- [ ] It loses its shape
- [ ] It stretches out of shape easily
- [ ] It droops, bags
- [x] It tends to wrinkle
- [ ] It resists wrinkles
- [ ] It crushes easily
- [ ] Water drops leave spots or marks

Suggested care
- [ ] Dryclean only
- [ ] Do not dryclean
- [x] Dryclean or wash
- [x] Gently handwash in lukewarm water
- [x] Roll in a towel to remove moisture
- [x] Drip dry
- [ ] Lay flat to dry
- [ ] Machine wash
  - [ ] gentle/delicate
  - [ ] regular/normal
  - [ ] do not spin
- [ ] Machine dry
  - [ ] cool [ ] normal
  - [ ] perm. press
- [x] Press damp fabric
- [ ] Press dry fabric
- [x] Dry iron [ ] Steam
- [ ] Iron on wrong side
- [ ] Use a press cloth
- [ ] Use a needleboard
- [ ] Needs no ironing
- [ ] Do not iron
- [ ] Fabric may shrink
- [ ] May bleed or fade

Where to find
- [ ] Any fabric store
- [ ] Major chain store
- [x] Stores that carry high quality fabric
- [ ] Fabric club
- [x] Mail order
- [x] Wholesale supplier

ATTACH SAMPLE HERE

LENGTHWISE GRAIN

Spun silk broadcloth has a dull luster.

broadcloth

A soft, lightweight, cotton-like silk fabric with a dull luster and very fine crosswise ribs, made with a tight, plain weave, fine warp yarns and slightly heavier filling yarns. Yarns may have a slack or tight twist. Fabric has a soft, supple hand and a flat, smooth surface. It is frequently made of spun silk, which enhances the fabric's cotton-like appearance. Solid colors and stripes are common, and the fabric sometimes has small dobby designs. It is also called shirting silk. Fuji silk is one type of broadcloth made from spun silk.

Spun silk

Short fibers, called floss, noil, staple and waste, are carded and spun into yarn, much like cotton and wool. Short fibers come from cocoons that are broken, damaged or tangled and can't be unreeled, and from waste on the outside and inside of the cocoon. Spun yarns are duller, fuzzier and weaker than yarns made from long filament. Fabrics often look more like cotton or linen than silk. Spun silk does not wear as well as filament silk, and fabrics tend to fray and pill.

How to use

Silk broadcloth has a gentle drape that falls into soft flares. It is easy to cut and sew, and can be gathered or shirred into a soft fullness. Pressed pleats and other folds are sharp and crisp. Fabric makes an excellent pintucked, tailored dress shirt. It is durable and travels well. Choose fitted, semi-fitted or loose styles to make shirts, blouses and lightweight dresses, or use as an underlining to stabilize loosely woven coatings and other heavy fabrics.

---

broadcloth

Originally, any fabric made on a loom wider than 27 inches, the width of narrow cloth. When a cotton shirting from Great Britain was introduced into the United States in the early 1920s, it was dubbed broadcloth because the British "poplin" was thought to describe a heavier fabric.

cotton broadcloth

A fine, closely woven, lustrous cotton or cotton/polyester shirting fabric with a fine crosswise rib. Crosswise yarns in this plain weave are heavier and have less twist than the lengthwise yarns. Combed ply yarns are used in better grades. Combed singles or carded yarns are used in poorer grades.

poplin

A durable, tightly woven fabric with fine crosswise ribs formed by fine lengthwise yarns and heavier crosswise yarns. Similar to broadcloth, but ribs are heavier. Usually made of cotton, but may also be silk, wool, synthetic or a blend. Originally made with silk warp yarns and wool filling yarns.

Sewing rating
- ☒ Easy to sew
- ☐ Moderately easy
- ☐ Average
- ☐ Moderately difficult
- ☐ Extremely difficult

Suggested fit
- ☐ Stretch to fit
- ☐ Close-fitting
- ☒ Fitted
- ☒ Semi-fitted
- ☒ Loose-fitting
- ☐ Very loose-fitting

Suggested styles
- ☒ Pleats ☒ Tucks
  - ☒ pressed
  - ☐ unpressed
- ☒ Gathers
  - ☐ limp ☒ soft
  - ☐ full ☐ lofty
  - ☐ bouffant
- ☒ Elasticized shirring
- ☒ Smocked
- ☒ Tailored
- ☐ Shaped with seams to eliminate bulk
- ☐ Lined
- ☐ Unlined
- ☐ Puffed or bouffant
- ☐ Loose and full
- ☐ Soft and flowing
- ☐ Draped
- ☐ Cut on bias
- ☐ Stretch styling

What to expect
- ☐ Fabric is slippery, difficult to control
- ☒ It is easy to cut out
- ☐ Difficult to cut out
- ☐ Fabric has a nap
- ☒ Fabric is reversible
- ☒ Both sides of fabric look the same
- ☐ It stretches easily
- ☐ It will not stretch
- ☒ It is difficult to ease sleeves and curves
- ☒ Fabric tears easily
- ☐ It is difficult to tear
- ☐ Fabric will not tear
- ☐ Pins and needles leave holes, marks
- ☐ It tends to pucker
- ☐ It tends to unravel
- ☐ Fabric won't unravel
- ☐ Inner construction shows from outside
- ☐ Machine eats fabric
- ☐ Skipped stitches
- ☐ Layers feed unevenly
- ☒ It creases easily
- ☐ Won't hold a crease

Cost per yard
- ☒ Less than $10
- ☒ $10 to $20
- ☐ $20 to $30
- ☐ $30 to $40
- ☐ $40 to $50
- ☐ More than $50

The rib weave

Rib fabrics are made with the plain weave, but the warp-to-filling ratio is changed so that one is heavier than the other. The prominent yarns conceal the smaller yarns, forming ribs. The prominent yarns may be heavier, or several yarns may be grouped and woven as one yarn. When the warp yarns are heavier, lengthwise cords are formed. Crosswise ribs are produced by prominent filling yarns. The smaller yarns are subject to abrasion and fabrics with prominent ribs tend to unravel. Ribbed silk fabrics include bengaline, faille, ottoman and poplin.

Wearability
- ☒ Durable ☐ Fragile
- ☐ Strong ☐ Weak
- ☒ It is long-wearing
- ☒ It wears evenly
- ☐ It wears out along seams and folds
- ☐ Seams don't hold up under stress
- ☐ Fabric is subject to abrasion
- ☐ It resists abrasion
- ☐ Subject to snags
- ☒ It resists snags
- ☐ Subject to runs
- ☒ It tends to pill
- ☐ It tends to shed
- ☐ It attracts lint
- ☐ It attracts static
- ☐ It is static-free
- ☐ It tends to cling
- ☒ It holds its shape
- ☐ It loses its shape
- ☐ It stretches out of shape easily
- ☐ It droops, bags
- ☒ It tends to wrinkle
- ☐ It resists wrinkles
- ☐ It crushes easily
- ☐ Water drops leave spots or marks

Suggested care
- ☐ Dryclean only
- ☐ Do not dryclean
- ☒ Dryclean or wash
- ☒ Gently handwash in lukewarm water
- ☒ Roll in a towel to remove moisture
- ☒ Drip dry
- ☐ Lay flat to dry
- ☐ Machine wash
  - ☐ gentle/delicate
  - ☐ regular/normal
  - ☐ do not spin
- ☐ Machine dry
  - ☐ cool ☐ normal
  - ☐ perm. press
- ☒ Press damp fabric
- ☐ Press dry fabric
- ☒ Dry iron ☐ Steam
- ☐ Iron on wrong side
- ☐ Use a press cloth
- ☐ Use a needleboard
- ☐ Needs no ironing
- ☐ Do not iron
- ☐ Fabric may shrink
- ☐ May bleed or fade

Where to find
- ☐ Any fabric store
- ☐ Major chain store
- ☒ Stores that carry high quality fabric
- ☒ Fabric club
- ☒ Mail order
- ☒ Wholesale supplier

ATTACH SAMPLE HERE

LENGTHWISE GRAIN

Brocade's prominent floats snag easily.

brocade

A rich, elegant fabric with a complex pattern woven on a jacquard loom with an extra set of yarns. Fabric has a stiff, heavy hand and a high/low relief pattern, usually of satin or twill floats, woven into a twill, satin or plain background weave. The floats snag easily and fabric is subject to abrasion. Brocade is usually woven with yarns of more than one color, and is medium to heavy in weight. It was originally woven in China and Japan of silk, with gold and silver threads. Today, all-silk brocade is very expensive and difficult to find. Blends are more common.

How to use

Silk brocade has a stiff drape that falls into wide cones. Fabric holds the shape of the garment and does not pleat or gather well. It works best in styles that are shaped with seams to eliminate bulk. A lining protects loose floats from getting caught on fingernails or heels. Choose close-fitting, fitted or semi-fitted styles to make jackets, skirts and evening wear. Use heavier fabrics for interior decorating. Dryclean to avoid snags and abrasions.

Damask

Brocade is frequently confused with its cousin, damask. Both fabrics have complicated floral or figured patterns woven on a jacquard loom. But damask is flatter than brocade and has shorter satin floats that do not snag as easily. Damask is usually reversible; brocade is not. Brocade is woven with several colors, while damask is usually a single color, with a dull-and-lustrous pattern that reverses itself on the flip side. Damask is often made of linen and used to make tablecloths.

---

brocatelle
Similar to brocade, but with a distinctive blistered or puffed appearance, often made of silk and used to make dresses. A heavier version of brocatelle is made with a silk warp and a different filling, usually of rayon or cotton. It is used to make draperies and upholstery.

brocatine
This brocade's design imitates embroidery.

broché
Brocade with a hand-embroidered design.

imperial brocade
Woven with real gold and silver threads.

tapestry
Similar to brocade, but usually heavier, with decorative designs depicting historical or current scenes instead of floral designs. Originally handwoven in the Orient. Today, tapestry-like fabrics are woven on the jacquard loom, and the distinction between tapestry and brocade has become blurred.

Sewing rating
- ☐ Easy to sew
- ☐ Moderately easy
- ☒ Average
- ☐ Moderately difficult
- ☐ Extremely difficult

Suggested fit
- ☐ Stretch to fit
- ☒ Close-fitting
- ☒ Fitted
- ☒ Semi-fitted
- ☐ Loose-fitting
- ☐ Very loose-fitting

Suggested styles
- ☐ Pleats ☐ Tucks
  - ☐ pressed
  - ☐ unpressed
- ☐ Gathers
  - ☐ limp ☐ soft
  - ☐ full ☐ lofty
  - ☐ bouffant
- ☐ Elasticized shirring
- ☐ Smocked
- ☐ Tailored
- ☒ Shaped with seams to eliminate bulk
- ☒ Lined
- ☐ Unlined
- ☐ Puffed or bouffant
- ☐ Loose and full
- ☐ Soft and flowing
- ☐ Draped
- ☐ Cut on bias
- ☐ Stretch styling

What to expect
- ☐ Fabric is slippery, difficult to control
- ☒ It is easy to cut out
- ☐ Difficult to cut out
- ☐ Fabric has a nap
- ☐ Fabric is reversible
- ☐ Both sides of fabric look the same
- ☐ It stretches easily
- ☐ It will not stretch
- ☒ It is difficult to ease sleeves and curves
- ☐ Fabric tears easily
- ☐ It is difficult to tear
- ☒ Fabric will not tear
- ☐ Pins and needles leave holes, marks
- ☐ It tends to pucker
- ☒ It tends to unravel
- ☐ Fabric won't unravel
- ☐ Inner construction shows from outside
- ☐ Machine eats fabric
- ☐ Skipped stitches
- ☒ Layers feed unevenly
- ☐ It creases easily
- ☒ Won't hold a crease

Cost per yard
- ☐ Less than $10
- ☐ $10 to $20
- ☐ $20 to $30
- ☒ $30 to $40
- ☒ $40 to $50
- ☒ More than $50

When to dryclean silk
Some silk fabrics, like brocade, should never be laundered at home. Other fabrics may be washable, but the garment style is not. Watch out for:
- ■ Loose weaves and long satin floats that snag.
- ■ Embossed fabrics and special finishes.
- ■ Slubbed or heavily ribbed fabrics that unravel.
- ■ Fabrics that tend to shrink.
- ■ Bright colors or prints that may bleed or fade.
- ■ Linings, shoulder pads and inner construction.
- ■ Fabrics that have special embellishments.
- ■ Fabrics like taffeta that are difficult to iron.
- ■ Unstable fabrics that are subject to yarn and seam slippage.

SIZE 8
100% SILK/SOIE MADE IN CHINA/ FAIT EN CHINE
DRYCLEAN ONLY

Wearability
- ☐ Durable ☒ Fragile
- ☐ Strong ☐ Weak
- ☐ It is long-wearing
- ☐ It wears evenly
- ☐ It wears out along seams and folds
- ☐ Seams don't hold up under stress
- ☒ Fabric is subject to abrasion
- ☐ It resists abrasion
- ☒ Subject to snags
- ☐ It resists snags
- ☐ Subject to runs
- ☐ It tends to pill

- ☐ It tends to shed
- ☐ It attracts lint
- ☐ It attracts static
- ☐ It is static-free
- ☐ It tends to cling
- ☒ It holds its shape
- ☐ It loses its shape
- ☐ It stretches out of shape easily
- ☐ It droops, bags
- ☐ It tends to wrinkle
- ☒ It resists wrinkles
- ☐ It crushes easily
- ☒ Water drops leave spots or marks

Suggested care
- ☒ Dryclean only
- ☐ Do not dryclean
- ☐ Dryclean or wash
- ☐ Gently handwash in lukewarm water
- ☐ Roll in a towel to remove moisture
- ☐ Drip dry
- ☐ Lay flat to dry
- ☐ Machine wash
  - ☐ gentle/delicate
  - ☐ regular/normal
  - ☐ do not spin
- ☐ Machine dry
  - ☐ cool ☐ normal
  - ☐ perm. press
- ☐ Press damp fabric
- ☐ Press dry fabric
- ☒ Dry iron ☐ Steam
- ☒ Iron on wrong side
- ☒ Use a press cloth
- ☐ Use a needleboard
- ☐ Needs no ironing
- ☐ Do not iron
- ☐ Fabric may shrink
- ☐ May bleed or fade

Where to find
- ☐ Any fabric store
- ☐ Major chain store
- ☒ Stores that carry high quality fabric
- ☐ Fabric club
- ☒ Mail order
- ☒ Wholesale supplier

ATTACH SAMPLE HERE

LENGTHWISE GRAIN

Lustrous charmeuse has a dull back.

charmeuse

A soft, elegant fabric with a softly lustrous face and a dull back, made with a satin weave, tightly twisted warp yarns and crepe or spun filling yarns. This popular fabric has a firm, soft, supple hand and a beautiful drape, but it snags, creases and scuffs easily. Once regarded as a luxury fabric, charmeuse is now one of the most common silks, available in weights ranging from 10mm to 18mm or more. Heavier versions are especially luxurious, and usually more expensive.

How to use

Silk charmeuse has a beautiful drape that falls close to the body in soft flares. It can be gathered into a soft fullness. Fabric tends to cling, and its lustrous, reflective surface may make the wearer appear heavier. Choose semi-fitted, loose or very loose, voluminous styles of blouses, dresses, evening wear, nightgowns and lingerie. It is sometimes used for lining. Use a very fine, sharp needle with no nicks or burrs to reduce snags. Luster may require a "with nap" layout. Drycleaning is recommended to avoid scuffs and abrasions.

Lustrous or dull

A fabric's luster is determined by its ability to reflect light. A flat, smooth surface, like a still body of water, produces a clear reflection. A textured surface, like ripples on water, produces a broken or distorted reflection, or no reflection at all. Tightly twisted and/or spun yarns are not very lustrous because each twist or break in the fiber adds a "ripple" to the fabric. Satin has fewer "ripples" than other weaves because the warp yarns float across the fabric, with fewer dips below the surface.

---

crepe-backed satin

A reversible satin fabric with a smooth, lustrous face and a dull, crepey back. Also called satin-backed crepe or satin crepe.

crepe charmeuse

Has tightly twisted crepe filling yarns, giving the back a slight crepe-like texture.

sandwashed charmeuse

Charmeuse that has been treated to an abrasive wash, using sand and chemicals, to produce a washable fabric with a soft, velvety hand, a supple bounce and a dulled luster. It is one of the most popular sandwashed silks. Also called silk chamois, doe silk, sueded silk and silk mousse.

satin charmeuse

Charmeuse made with spun filling yarns, producing fabric with a plain, dull back.

satin merveilleux

French for "marvelous." A soft silk fabric with a very high luster, often woven with two colors for an iridescent effect.

Sewing rating

- [ ] Easy to sew
- [ ] Moderately easy
- [x] Average
- [ ] Moderately difficult
- [ ] Extremely difficult

Suggested fit

- [ ] Stretch to fit
- [ ] Close-fitting
- [ ] Fitted
- [x] Semi-fitted
- [x] Loose-fitting
- [x] Very loose-fitting

Suggested styles

- [ ] Pleats [ ] Tucks
  - [ ] pressed
  - [ ] unpressed
- [x] Gathers
  - [ ] limp [x] soft
  - [ ] full [ ] lofty
  - [ ] bouffant
- [x] Elasticized shirring
- [ ] Smocked
- [ ] Tailored
- [ ] Shaped with seams to eliminate bulk
- [ ] Lined
- [ ] Unlined
- [ ] Puffed or bouffant
- [x] Loose and full
- [x] Soft and flowing
- [x] Draped
- [x] Cut on bias
- [ ] Stretch styling

What to expect

- [x] Fabric is slippery, difficult to control
- [ ] It is easy to cut out
- [x] Difficult to cut out
- [x] Fabric has a nap
- [ ] Fabric is reversible
- [ ] Both sides of fabric look the same
- [ ] It stretches easily
- [ ] It will not stretch
- [ ] It is difficult to ease sleeves and curves
- [x] Fabric tears easily
- [ ] It is difficult to tear
- [ ] Fabric will not tear
- [x] Pins and needles leave holes, marks
- [ ] It tends to pucker
- [ ] It tends to unravel
- [x] Fabric won't unravel
- [ ] Inner construction shows from outside
- [ ] Machine eats fabric
- [ ] Skipped stitches
- [ ] Layers feed unevenly
- [x] It creases easily
- [ ] Won't hold a crease

Cost per yard

- [ ] Less than $10
- [x] $10 to $20
- [x] $20 to $30
- [x] $30 to $40
- [ ] $40 to $50
- [ ] More than $50

The satin weave

Satin is the most fragile of the three basic weaves, made by weaving long warp "floats" over four or more filling yarns, under one, then over four more in a varied, random pattern. It is usually woven with lustrous filament yarns, such as silk, that have little or no twist, resulting in fabric with a lustrous, reflective surface that ranges from a dull sheen to a high gloss. The satin weave is also used to produce a number of other fabrics that do not look like satin and have different names, but all satin and satin-weave fabrics have long floats that tend to snag.

Wearability

- [ ] Durable [x] Fragile
- [ ] Strong [ ] Weak
- [ ] It is long-wearing
- [ ] It wears evenly
- [ ] It wears out along seams and folds
- [ ] Seams don't hold up under stress
- [x] Fabric is subject to abrasion
- [ ] It resists abrasion
- [x] Subject to snags
- [ ] It resists snags
- [ ] Subject to runs
- [ ] It tends to pill
- [ ] It tends to shed
- [ ] It attracts lint
- [x] It attracts static
- [ ] It is static-free
- [x] It tends to cling
- [ ] It holds its shape
- [ ] It loses its shape
- [ ] It stretches out of shape easily
- [ ] It droops, bags
- [x] It tends to wrinkle
- [ ] It resists wrinkles
- [ ] It crushes easily
- [x] Water drops leave spots or marks

Suggested care

- [x] Dryclean only
- [ ] Do not dryclean
- [ ] Dryclean or wash
- [ ] Gently handwash in lukewarm water
- [ ] Roll in a towel to remove moisture
- [ ] Drip dry
- [ ] Lay flat to dry
- [ ] Machine wash
  - [ ] gentle/delicate
  - [ ] regular/normal
  - [ ] do not spin
- [ ] Machine dry
  - [ ] cool [ ] normal
  - [ ] perm. press
- [ ] Press damp fabric
- [x] Press dry fabric
- [x] Dry iron [ ] Steam
- [x] Iron on wrong side
- [x] Use a press cloth
- [ ] Use a needleboard
- [ ] Needs no ironing
- [ ] Do not iron
- [ ] Fabric may shrink
- [ ] May bleed or fade

Where to find

- [ ] Any fabric store
- [x] Major chain store
- [x] Stores that carry high quality fabric
- [x] Fabric club
- [x] Mail order
- [x] Wholesale supplier

Chiffon is softer than georgette.

chiffon

French for "rag." Chiffon is indeed the ragdoll of silk fabrics. This elegant, sheer fabric is quite limp, with a soft, beautiful drape. It is made with a loose, plain weave and tightly twisted single yarns in both directions. It has a soft, supple, thin hand and a flat, crepe-like texture. Chiffon is very fine to lightweight (4mm to 6mm), but strong. It is often confused with georgette, but chiffon is softer, thinner and has less crepe. It is often treated with special starches, which cause spots to appear if it gets wet (avoid steam irons and rainstorms).

How to use

Chiffon has a graceful drape that falls into soft, languid flares and ripples. It can be gathered or shirred into a limp fullness. The fabric is extremely difficult to cut and sew; it is slippery and snags easily. Seams, facings and hems can be seen from the finished side of the garment. Use to make special occasion dresses, scarves and nightgowns, or for linings and underlinings. Drycleaning is recommended. A good drycleaner can remove water spots.

Soft and sheer

The term "chiffon" is frequently paired with other fabric names to indicate a soft, lightweight or transparent version of the other cloth, which has little or no resemblance to real chiffon. For example, chiffon taffeta is soft, lustrous, very lightweight taffeta. Chiffon velvet is very soft and almost transparent. It is also called wedding ring velvet, supposedly because a garment of the fabric can be pulled through a ring. "Paper" and "tissue" are also used to describe lightweight fabrics.

---

crepe chiffon
Used to describe chiffon and georgette.

satin-striped chiffon
Chiffon with lustrous stripes of satin.

chiffonette
A very soft, lightweight version of chiffon.

gauze
A term often used loosely to describe silk chiffon and organza, but authentic gauze is made with a variation of the leno weave, which laces pairs of warp yarns around the filling yarns in a figure 8 arrangement. This adds strength and stability to loose, open weaves and prevents yarns from slipping.

mousseline de soie
French for "silk muslin," although the fabric it describes is finer than muslin, which is usually made of cotton. This version is a lightweight, sheer, plain-weave fabric that resembles chiffon, but is firmer and has more body. Like chiffon, it is often finished with sizing, but the amount varies.

Sewing rating
- ☐ Easy to sew
- ☐ Moderately easy
- ☐ Average
- ☐ Moderately difficult
- ☒ Extremely difficult

Suggested fit
- ☐ Stretch to fit
- ☐ Close-fitting
- ☐ Fitted
- ☐ Semi-fitted
- ☒ Loose-fitting
- ☒ Very loose-fitting

Suggested styles
- ☐ Pleats ☐ Tucks
  - ☐ pressed
  - ☐ unpressed
- ☒ Gathers
  - ☒ limp ☐ soft
  - ☐ full ☐ lofty
  - ☐ bouffant
- ☒ Elasticized shirring
- ☐ Smocked
- ☐ Tailored
- ☐ Shaped with seams to eliminate bulk
- ☒ Lined
- ☐ Unlined
- ☐ Puffed or bouffant
- ☒ Loose and full
- ☒ Soft and flowing
- ☒ Draped
- ☒ Cut on bias
- ☐ Stretch styling

What to expect
- ☒ Fabric is slippery, difficult to control
- ☐ It is easy to cut out
- ☒ Difficult to cut out
- ☐ Fabric has a nap
- ☒ Fabric is reversible
- ☒ Both sides of fabric look the same
- ☐ It stretches easily
- ☐ It will not stretch
- ☐ It is difficult to ease sleeves and curves
- ☒ Fabric tears easily
- ☐ It is difficult to tear
- ☐ Fabric will not tear
- ☐ Pins and needles leave holes, marks
- ☒ It tends to pucker
- ☐ It tends to unravel
- ☐ Fabric won't unravel
- ☒ Inner construction shows from outside
- ☒ Machine eats fabric
- ☐ Skipped stitches
- ☐ Layers feed unevenly
- ☐ It creases easily
- ☒ Won't hold a crease

Cost per yard
- ☐ Less than $10
- ☒ $10 to $20
- ☒ $20 to $30
- ☒ $30 to $40
- ☐ $40 to $50
- ☐ More than $50

A 'single' yarn isn't really
Nothing compares in sheerness to a fine, filmy fabric made from single silk yarns, such as chiffon. But the term "single" is misleading. The silkworm spins a double strand of silk that is held together by a natural silk gum called sericin. The very finest silk yarns are made from two of these double strands, unwound from two cocoons and reeled together into a single yarn. Reeled silk is measured in deniers (one denier equals 0.05 grams per 450 meter length). A double silk filament is about 2 deniers, so the finest single yarn is 4 to 5 deniers. For comparison, an average silk yarn is about 13 to 15 deniers.

Wearability
- ☒ Durable ☐ Fragile
- ☒ Strong ☐ Weak
- ☐ It is long-wearing
- ☒ It wears evenly
- ☐ It wears out along seams and folds
- ☐ Seams don't hold up under stress
- ☐ Fabric is subject to abrasion
- ☐ It resists abrasion
- ☒ Subject to snags
- ☐ It resists snags
- ☐ Subject to runs
- ☐ It tends to pill

- ☐ It tends to shed
- ☐ It attracts lint
- ☐ It attracts static
- ☐ It is static-free
- ☐ It tends to cling
- ☐ It holds its shape
- ☐ It loses its shape
- ☐ It stretches out of shape easily
- ☐ It droops, bags
- ☐ It tends to wrinkle
- ☒ It resists wrinkles
- ☐ It crushes easily
- ☒ Water drops leave spots or marks

Suggested care
- ☒ Dryclean only
- ☐ Do not dryclean
- ☐ Dryclean or wash
- ☐ Gently handwash in lukewarm water
- ☐ Roll in a towel to remove moisture
- ☐ Drip dry
- ☐ Lay flat to dry
- ☐ Machine wash
  - ☐ gentle/delicate
  - ☐ regular/normal
  - ☐ do not spin
- ☐ Machine dry
  - ☐ cool ☐ normal
  - ☐ perm. press
- ☐ Press damp fabric
- ☒ Press dry fabric
- ☒ Dry iron ☐ Steam
- ☐ Iron on wrong side
- ☐ Use a press cloth
- ☐ Use a needleboard
- ☐ Needs no ironing
- ☐ Do not iron
- ☒ Fabric may shrink
- ☐ May bleed or fade

Where to find
- ☐ Any fabric store
- ☐ Major chain store
- ☒ Stores that carry high quality fabric
- ☐ Fabric club
- ☒ Mail order
- ☒ Wholesale supplier

China silk

A soft, lightweight, lustrous silk made with a tight, plain weave and very fine yarns, originally handwoven in China of hand-reeled silk. Fabric has a limp, soft, thin hand and a slippery, smooth texture. It varies in weight from 5mm to 10mm, but 8mm is the most popular. China silk is sometimes called habutai, but authentic habutai is usually slightly irregular and is natural in color, while China silk is smoother and is frequently dyed. China silk is one of the least expensive and most common silks on the market today.

How to use

China silk has a soft, graceful drape that falls into languid flares. It can be gathered into a limp fullness. Fabric is slippery, fairly delicate and not very durable. It tends to snag, it wears poorly and it is subject to yarn and seam slippage, so it is wise to avoid close-fitting styles that put stress on seams. Choose semi-fitted, loose-fitting or very loose-fitting styles to make lingerie, lightweight blouses, linings and underlinings. Dryclean or gently wash by hand.

Weighted silk

Silk loses up to 25 percent of its weight when the natural silk gum, called sericin, is removed. Because silk is sold by weight, it was once common practice to restore some of the weight by adding metallic salts, such as lead, tin or iron. Such weighting "improved" the silk's quality and disguised inferior fabrics. But weighted silk tends to crack, and heavy salts, especially lead, proved to be harmful to people, so the practice fell out of favor. Most silk sold in the United States today is not weighted.

---

corah silk

A lightweight silk fabric made in India from natural colored, raw silk. After weaving, the fabric is degummed, leaving a creamy white color. The fabric was originally made of wild silk, but today it is usually of cultivated silk and is often dyed or printed. The name is derived from the Hindu word for virgin.

Fuji silk

A type of broadcloth made from spun silk.

Indian silk

Another name for sari silk.

Jap silk

Another name for China silk and habutai.

sari silk

A very fine, filmy, plain-weave silk fabric handwoven in India and used to make saris. Fabric is similar to the original, handwoven China silk. It has a beautiful natural luster and whiteness, which make it ideal for dyeing. Typically has weaving irregularities about every 4 inches, and is loosely woven.

Sewing rating
- [ ] Easy to sew
- [ ] Moderately easy
- [x] Average
- [ ] Moderately difficult
- [ ] Extremely difficult

Suggested fit
- [ ] Stretch to fit
- [ ] Close-fitting
- [ ] Fitted
- [ ] Semi-fitted
- [x] Loose-fitting
- [x] Very loose-fitting

Suggested styles
- [x] Pleats [x] Tucks
  - [x] pressed
  - [ ] unpressed
- [x] Gathers
  - [x] limp [x] soft
  - [ ] full [ ] lofty
  - [ ] bouffant
- [ ] Elasticized shirring
- [ ] Smocked
- [ ] Tailored
- [ ] Shaped with seams to eliminate bulk
- [ ] Lined
- [ ] Unlined
- [ ] Puffed or bouffant
- [x] Loose and full
- [x] Soft and flowing
- [x] Draped
- [ ] Cut on bias
- [ ] Stretch styling

What to expect
- [ ] Fabric is slippery, difficult to control
- [ ] It is easy to cut out
- [ ] Difficult to cut out
- [ ] Fabric has a nap
- [x] Fabric is reversible
- [x] Both sides of fabric look the same
- [ ] It stretches easily
- [ ] It will not stretch
- [ ] It is difficult to ease sleeves and curves
- [x] Fabric tears easily
- [ ] It is difficult to tear
- [ ] Fabric will not tear
- [ ] Pins and needles leave holes, marks
- [ ] It tends to pucker
- [ ] It tends to unravel
- [ ] Fabric won't unravel
- [ ] Inner construction shows from outside
- [ ] Machine eats fabric
- [ ] Skipped stitches
- [ ] Layers feed unevenly
- [x] It creases easily
- [ ] Won't hold a crease

Cost per yard
- [x] Less than $10
- [x] $10 to $20
- [ ] $20 to $30
- [ ] $30 to $40
- [ ] $40 to $50
- [ ] More than $50

Silk from China
Silk was officially discovered in about 2640 B.C., when a Chinese empress accidentally dropped a cocoon into her bath. The hot water softened the cocoon, causing it to unravel. The empress was so impressed with the wispy, lustrous fibers that she put the imperial weavers to work. China managed to keep the source of silk a secret for several thousand years, while it busily exported silk goods to the West along the fabled "silk road." Eventually, silkworm eggs, sericulture methods and weaving techniques were smuggled out of the country. Today, China shares the market, but still produces the most silk – about 50 percent.

Wearability
- [ ] Durable [x] Fragile
- [ ] Strong [x] Weak
- [ ] It is long-wearing
- [ ] It wears evenly
- [ ] It wears out along seams and folds
- [x] Seams don't hold up under stress
- [ ] Fabric is subject to abrasion
- [ ] It resists abrasion
- [x] Subject to snags
- [ ] It resists snags
- [ ] Subject to runs
- [ ] It tends to pill
- [ ] It tends to shed
- [ ] It attracts lint
- [ ] It attracts static
- [ ] It is static-free
- [ ] It tends to cling
- [ ] It holds its shape
- [ ] It loses its shape
- [ ] It stretches out of shape easily
- [ ] It droops, bags
- [x] It tends to wrinkle
- [ ] It resists wrinkles
- [ ] It crushes easily
- [ ] Water drops leave spots or marks

Suggested care
- [ ] Dryclean only
- [ ] Do not dryclean
- [x] Dryclean or wash
- [x] Gently handwash in lukewarm water
- [x] Roll in a towel to remove moisture
- [x] Drip dry
- [ ] Lay flat to dry
- [ ] Machine wash
  - [ ] gentle/delicate
  - [ ] regular/normal
  - [ ] do not spin
- [ ] Machine dry
  - [ ] cool [ ] normal
  - [ ] perm. press
- [x] Press damp fabric
- [ ] Press dry fabric
- [x] Dry iron [ ] Steam
- [ ] Iron on wrong side
- [ ] Use a press cloth
- [ ] Use a needleboard
- [ ] Needs no ironing
- [ ] Do not iron
- [x] Fabric may shrink
- [ ] May bleed or fade

Where to find
- [ ] Any fabric store
- [x] Major chain store
- [x] Stores that carry high quality fabric
- [x] Fabric club
- [x] Mail order
- [x] Wholesale supplier

ATTACH SAMPLE HERE

LENGTHWISE GRAIN

Silk cloqué has a blistered pattern.

cloqué

French for "blistered." A soft, lightweight crepe fabric with a puckered, sculptured or blistered effect on the surface, similar to matelassé but not made the same way. Fabric has a firm hand and a high/low relief pattern that has lustrous and dull areas. Some versions are made with a modified double-cloth construction, while others are embossed or treated with a special finish to produce the raised effect. Cloqué is usually silk, but it may also be rayon or polyester. The term is also used more loosely to describe any fabric with a puckered or blistered surface, including matelassé. Also called embossed jacquard.

How to use

Cloqué is an elegant fabric with a beautiful drape that falls close to the body in soft ripples and flares. It may be gathered into a soft fullness. Fabric may be quite slippery and is moderately difficult to sew. Choose semi-fitted, loose-fitting or very loose-fitting styles to make blouses, dresses and evening wear. Drycleaning is recommended because cloqué, like all crepes, tends to shrink.

Embossed fabric

Fabric is embossed by passing it through a series of heated, engraved rollers, much like a newspaper is printed. Figures and designs are transferred to the fabric when pressure is applied under carefully monitored conditions. Finished fabrics have blistered, raised, puckered or sculptured designs. This technique is often used to change the characteristics of crepe, satin and velvet fabrics. It is usually permanent on synthetics, but may wear off or wash out of silks and rayons.

---

blister cloth
A broad term for fabrics with a blistered surface, including cloqué and matelassé.

blister crepe
A fine, combed lawn or print cloth treated with a caustic soda, which shrinks part of the cloth, producing blisters in the design.

cloky
The Americanized spelling of cloqué. The French spelling is preferred.

puckered cloth
Used to describe fabric with a blistered, crinkled or puffed effect that is sometimes desired and sometimes a fabric fault.

wool cloqué
A fine, wool double cloth with a blistered or raised surface. Mohair is used for the top layer and botany wool for the bottom layer. The botany wool shrinks during finishing, but the mohair does not, causing the mohair yarns to blister or pucker up. The mohair side is used as the face.

Sewing rating
- [ ] Easy to sew
- [ ] Moderately easy
- [ ] Average
- [x] Moderately difficult
- [ ] Extremely difficult

Suggested fit
- [ ] Stretch to fit
- [ ] Close-fitting
- [ ] Fitted
- [x] Semi-fitted
- [x] Loose-fitting
- [x] Very loose-fitting

Suggested styles
- [ ] Pleats [ ] Tucks
  - [ ] pressed
  - [ ] unpressed
- [x] Gathers
  - [ ] limp [x] soft
  - [ ] full [ ] lofty
  - [ ] bouffant
- [ ] Elasticized shirring
- [ ] Smocked
- [ ] Tailored
- [ ] Shaped with seams to eliminate bulk
- [ ] Lined
- [ ] Unlined
- [ ] Puffed or bouffant
- [x] Loose and full
- [x] Soft and flowing
- [x] Draped
- [ ] Cut on bias
- [ ] Stretch styling

What to expect
- [x] Fabric is slippery, difficult to control
- [ ] It is easy to cut out
- [ ] Difficult to cut out
- [ ] Fabric has a nap
- [ ] Fabric is reversible
- [ ] Both sides of fabric look the same
- [ ] It stretches easily
- [ ] It will not stretch
- [ ] It is difficult to ease sleeves and curves
- [ ] Fabric tears easily
- [ ] It is difficult to tear
- [x] Fabric will not tear
- [ ] Pins and needles leave holes, marks
- [ ] It tends to pucker
- [ ] It tends to unravel
- [ ] Fabric won't unravel
- [ ] Inner construction shows from outside
- [ ] Machine eats fabric
- [ ] Skipped stitches
- [ ] Layers feed unevenly
- [ ] It creases easily
- [x] Won't hold a crease

Cost per yard
- [ ] Less than $10
- [ ] $10 to $20
- [ ] $20 to $30
- [x] $30 to $40
- [x] $40 to $50
- [ ] More than $50

French influence
A quick glance at the fabrics in this book is all it takes to realize that France played a key role in the history of silk. During the Renaissance, France established itself as a center for silk weaving, especially the area around Lyon. Then, in the mid-19th century, disaster struck in the form of a deadly silkworm disease, and the French silk industry was almost wiped out. Scientist Louis Pasteur, better known for his development of pasteurized milk, was called into action. He developed a way to identify and eliminate diseased silk moths and their eggs. His "cure" is still used today, and Pasteur is regarded by some as the savior of the silk industry.

Wearability
- [ ] Durable [ ] Fragile
- [x] Strong [ ] Weak
- [ ] It is long-wearing
- [ ] It wears evenly
- [ ] It wears out along seams and folds
- [ ] Seams don't hold up under stress
- [x] Fabric is subject to abrasion
- [ ] It resists abrasion
- [x] Subject to snags
- [ ] It resists snags
- [ ] Subject to runs
- [ ] It tends to pill
- [ ] It tends to shed
- [ ] It attracts lint
- [ ] It attracts static
- [ ] It is static-free
- [ ] It tends to cling
- [x] It holds its shape
- [ ] It loses its shape
- [ ] It stretches out of shape easily
- [ ] It droops, bags
- [ ] It tends to wrinkle
- [x] It resists wrinkles
- [ ] It crushes easily
- [x] Water drops leave spots or marks

Suggested care
- [x] Dryclean only
- [ ] Do not dryclean
- [ ] Dryclean or wash
- [ ] Gently handwash in lukewarm water
- [ ] Roll in a towel to remove moisture
- [ ] Drip dry
- [ ] Lay flat to dry
- [ ] Machine wash
  - [ ] gentle/delicate
  - [ ] regular/normal
  - [ ] do not spin
- [ ] Machine dry
  - [ ] cool [ ] normal
  - [ ] perm. press
- [ ] Press damp fabric
- [ ] Press dry fabric
- [ ] Dry iron [ ] Steam
- [ ] Iron on wrong side
- [ ] Use a press cloth
- [ ] Use a needleboard
- [x] Needs no ironing
- [ ] Do not iron
- [x] Fabric may shrink
- [x] May bleed or fade

Where to find
- [ ] Any fabric store
- [ ] Major chain store
- [x] Stores that carry high quality fabric
- [ ] Fabric club
- [x] Mail order
- [x] Wholesale supplier

ATTACH SAMPLE HERE

LENGTHWISE GRAIN

Silk crepe has a crinkled texture.

crepe

Expensive, luxurious fabric with a dull sheen and slight crosswise ribs, formed by fine warp yarns and slightly heavier filling yarns. Crepe is usually made with a plain weave and alternating S- and Z-twist crepe yarns in both directions. The soft, pliable fabric has a crinkly, pebbled texture that may be almost smooth or quite rough. Crepe is heavier and more textured than crepe de Chine, but not as slippery. The heaviest, most luxurious fabrics are made from three- or four-ply yarns.

Why silk shrinks

Silk fiber does not shrink, but many silk fabrics, like crepe, shrink a little or a lot. This is because of the way the fabric is made. Plain- and twill-weave fabrics are especially prone to shrinkage. High-twist yarns and loose weaves shrink more than low-twist yarns and tight weaves. Crepe, which is usually made with a plain weave and tightly twisted yarns, is a good candidate for shrinkage. A loosely woven crepe is almost guaranteed to shrink, even if it is made of silk.

How to use

Silk crepe has a beautiful drape that falls into soft, wide flares. It can be gathered into a moderate fullness, but pleats and tucks won't hold a crease. The fabric is moderately easy to cut and sew, but it tends to unravel and it stretches in the crosswise direction. Silk crepe is durable and wears well. Choose fitted, semi-fitted or loose-fitting styles to make dresses, slacks, skirts, lightweight suits, bridal gowns and evening wear. Dryclean or gently wash by hand, but beware: crepe fabrics tend to shrink a lot.

---

bark crepe
A rough crepe that resembles tree bark, usually made with silk or synthetic warp yarns and wool or rayon filling yarns.

Canton crepe
Made from Canton silk, a soft, lustrous silk that is weaker and very lightweight.

crepon
A heavy, rugged crepe fabric, usually made of silk or rayon and used to make dresses.

crepe marocain
A heavy crepe dress fabric of silk and/or rayon with crosswise ribs. Filling yarns are coarser than warp yarns.

rough crepe
Crepe with a pronounced rough or pebbled surface, made with high-twist yarns and a plain weave. A silk version is woven of raw silk, then degummed, dyed and finished. The most common version is made of acetate and rayon; other versions may be all-rayon, all-acetate, and sometimes, cotton.

Sewing rating
- [ ] Easy to sew
- [x] Moderately easy
- [ ] Average
- [ ] Moderately difficult
- [ ] Extremely difficult

Suggested fit
- [ ] Stretch to fit
- [ ] Close-fitting
- [x] Fitted
- [x] Semi-fitted
- [x] Loose-fitting
- [ ] Very loose-fitting

Suggested styles
- [ ] Pleats [x] Tucks
  - [ ] pressed
  - [x] unpressed
- [x] Gathers
  - [ ] limp [x] soft
  - [x] full [ ] lofty
  - [ ] bouffant
- [ ] Elasticized shirring
- [ ] Smocked
- [ ] Tailored
- [ ] Shaped with seams to eliminate bulk
- [ ] Lined
- [ ] Unlined
- [ ] Puffed or bouffant
- [x] Loose and full
- [ ] Soft and flowing
- [x] Draped
- [ ] Cut on bias
- [ ] Stretch styling

What to expect
- [ ] Fabric is slippery, difficult to control
- [ ] It is easy to cut out
- [ ] Difficult to cut out
- [ ] Fabric has a nap
- [x] Fabric is reversible
- [x] Both sides of fabric look the same
- [x] It stretches easily
- [ ] It will not stretch
- [ ] It is difficult to ease sleeves and curves
- [ ] Fabric tears easily
- [ ] It is difficult to tear
- [ ] Fabric will not tear
- [ ] Pins and needles leave holes, marks
- [ ] It tends to pucker
- [x] It tends to unravel
- [ ] Fabric won't unravel
- [ ] Inner construction shows from outside
- [ ] Machine eats fabric
- [ ] Skipped stitches
- [ ] Layers feed unevenly
- [ ] It creases easily
- [x] Won't hold a crease

Cost per yard
- [ ] Less than $10
- [ ] $10 to $20
- [ ] $20 to $30
- [x] $30 to $40
- [x] $40 to $50
- [x] More than $50

Crepe fabrics

Crepe fabrics have a crinkled or pebbled texture that may be fine and smooth, like crepe de Chine, or very rough and pronounced, like bark crepe. Authentic crepe fabrics are woven with tightly twisted crepe yarns in one or both directions. The tight twist reduces the silk's natural luster, which results in fabric with a dull surface. Crepe is usually made with the plain weave, but variations are made with twill, satin and jacquard weaves. Crepe-like fabrics are embossed or treated with a chemical finish, but the crepe effect is not always permanent.

Wearability
- [x] Durable [ ] Fragile
- [x] Strong [ ] Weak
- [x] It is long-wearing
- [x] It wears evenly
- [ ] It wears out along seams and folds
- [ ] Seams don't hold up under stress
- [ ] Fabric is subject to abrasion
- [ ] It resists abrasion
- [ ] Subject to snags
- [ ] It resists snags
- [ ] Subject to runs
- [ ] It tends to pill
- [ ] It tends to shed
- [ ] It attracts lint
- [ ] It attracts static
- [ ] It is static-free
- [ ] It tends to cling
- [ ] It holds its shape
- [ ] It loses its shape
- [x] It stretches out of shape easily
- [ ] It droops, bags
- [ ] It tends to wrinkle
- [x] It resists wrinkles
- [ ] It crushes easily
- [ ] Water drops leave spots or marks

Suggested care
- [ ] Dryclean only
- [ ] Do not dryclean
- [x] Dryclean or wash
- [x] Gently handwash in lukewarm water
- [x] Roll in a towel to remove moisture
- [ ] Drip dry
- [x] Lay flat to dry
- [ ] Machine wash
  - [ ] gentle/delicate
  - [ ] regular/normal
  - [ ] do not spin
- [ ] Machine dry
  - [ ] cool [ ] normal
  - [ ] perm. press
- [x] Press damp fabric
- [ ] Press dry fabric
- [x] Dry iron [ ] Steam
- [ ] Iron on wrong side
- [ ] Use a press cloth
- [ ] Use a needleboard
- [ ] Needs no ironing
- [ ] Do not iron
- [x] Fabric may shrink
- [x] May bleed or fade

Where to find
- [ ] Any fabric store
- [ ] Major chain store
- [x] Stores that carry high quality fabric
- [ ] Fabric club
- [x] Mail order
- [x] Wholesale supplier

ATTACH SAMPLE HERE

LENGTHWISE GRAIN

Crepe de Chine is flat and smooth.

crepe de Chine

French for "crepe from China." A lightweight, soft silk crepe made with a plain weave and alternating S- and Z-twist yarns in both the warp and filling. Fabric has a fine, firm hand and a somewhat lustrous, smooth, slippery surface. It is available in several weights: 14mm is common; 16mm is more luxurious and drapes beautifully. Crepe de Chine was once considered to be a luxury fabric, but it is now one of the most commonly available silks. It is usually more expensive than China silk. The most common synthetic version is made of polyester.

How to use

Crepe de Chine has a soft, graceful drape that falls into limp, soft ripples and flares. It can be gathered, tucked or shirred. Heavier versions may be pleated. Use a very fine, sharp needle with no nicks or burrs to avoid snags. Fabric tends to wrinkle, but smoothness is easily restored with a warm iron. Use to make semi-fitted, loose-fitting or very loose-fitting styles of blouses, shirts, lightweight dresses and lingerie. Dryclean or gently wash by hand.

Crepe yarns

Most yarns have some amount of twist because the twist is what holds the fibers together. The twist is either balanced or unbalanced. A balanced yarn is twisted so that the yarn does not twist, kink or double up when suspended in a loop. Balanced yarns are used to make smooth fabrics. An unbalanced yarn will untwist and retwist in the other direction when suspended in a loop. Unbalanced yarns are used to make textured and/or pebbly fabrics, like crepe, and are often called crepe yarns.

---

flat crepe
One of the smoothest crepe fabrics, made with a plain weave, ordinary twist warp yarns and tightly twisted S- and Z-twist crepe filling yarns. It usually has more filling yarns per inch than warps and is made of silk and/or synthetic fibers. Sometimes inaccurately called French crepe.

French crepe
Originally, the name given to a flat crepe made in France. Now, a lightweight, rayon or silk, plain-weave fabric that resembles flat crepe. The filling has more twist than the warp, but it is not a crepe twist, and all the yarns are twisted the same direction, producing a modified crepe effect.

Kabe crepe
A silk crepe de Chine with a slightly stiffer finish than usual, made in Japan.

mock crepe
Similar to flat crepe, but made without crepe yarns. The crepe effect is obtained by an unusual weave or a chemical finish.

Sewing rating
- ☐ Easy to sew
- ☐ Moderately easy
- ☒ Average
- ☐ Moderately difficult
- ☐ Extremely difficult

Suggested fit
- ☐ Stretch to fit
- ☐ Close-fitting
- ☐ Fitted
- ☒ Semi-fitted
- ☒ Loose-fitting
- ☒ Very loose-fitting

Suggested styles
- ☒ Pleats ☒ Tucks
  - ☒ pressed
  - ☐ unpressed
- ☒ Gathers
  - ☐ limp ☒ soft
  - ☐ full ☐ lofty
  - ☐ bouffant
- ☒ Elasticized shirring
- ☐ Smocked
- ☐ Tailored
- ☐ Shaped with seams to eliminate bulk
- ☐ Lined
- ☐ Unlined
- ☐ Puffed or bouffant
- ☒ Loose and full
- ☒ Soft and flowing
- ☒ Draped
- ☒ Cut on bias
- ☐ Stretch styling

What to expect
- ☒ Fabric is slippery, difficult to control
- ☐ It is easy to cut out
- ☒ Difficult to cut out
- ☐ Fabric has a nap
- ☒ Fabric is reversible
- ☒ Both sides of fabric look the same
- ☐ It stretches easily
- ☐ It will not stretch
- ☐ It is difficult to ease sleeves and curves
- ☒ Fabric tears easily
- ☐ It is difficult to tear
- ☐ Fabric will not tear
- ☐ Pins and needles leave holes, marks
- ☐ It tends to pucker
- ☐ It tends to unravel
- ☒ Fabric won't unravel
- ☐ Inner construction shows from outside
- ☐ Machine eats fabric
- ☐ Skipped stitches
- ☐ Layers feed unevenly
- ☒ It creases easily
- ☐ Won't hold a crease

Cost per yard
- ☐ Less than $10
- ☒ $10 to $20
- ☒ $20 to $30
- ☐ $30 to $40
- ☐ $40 to $50
- ☐ More than $50

Twisted yarns
Twist gives personality to yarn while holding it together. The yarn's twist can be in either direction: A clockwise, or right-hand, rotation produces a Z-twist yarn, while a left-hand, or counterclockwise, rotation produces an S-twist yarn. Different effects can be achieved by changing the amount of twist and its direction. For example, the three single strands of a triple-ply yarn may each be tightly twisted in one direction, then bound together with a loose twist in the other. A yarn of the same configuration will have different characteristics if the singles are not twisted at all before twisting them together.

Wearability
- ☒ Durable ☐ Fragile
- ☒ Strong ☐ Weak
- ☒ It is long-wearing
- ☒ It wears evenly
- ☐ It wears out along seams and folds
- ☐ Seams don't hold up under stress
- ☐ Fabric is subject to abrasion
- ☐ It resists abrasion
- ☒ Subject to snags
- ☐ It resists snags
- ☐ Subject to runs
- ☐ It tends to pill
- ☐ It tends to shed
- ☐ It attracts lint
- ☒ It attracts static
- ☐ It is static-free
- ☒ It tends to cling
- ☒ It holds its shape
- ☐ It loses its shape
- ☐ It stretches out of shape easily
- ☐ It droops, bags
- ☒ It tends to wrinkle
- ☐ It resists wrinkles
- ☐ It crushes easily
- ☐ Water drops leave spots or marks

Suggested care
- ☐ Dryclean only
- ☐ Do not dryclean
- ☒ Dryclean or wash
- ☒ Gently handwash in lukewarm water
- ☒ Roll in a towel to remove moisture
- ☒ Drip dry
- ☐ Lay flat to dry
- ☐ Machine wash
  - ☐ gentle/delicate
  - ☐ regular/normal
  - ☐ do not spin
- ☐ Machine dry
  - ☐ cool ☐ normal
  - ☐ perm. press
- ☒ Press damp fabric
- ☐ Press dry fabric
- ☒ Dry iron ☐ Steam
- ☐ Iron on wrong side
- ☐ Use a press cloth
- ☐ Use a needleboard
- ☐ Needs no ironing
- ☐ Do not iron
- ☒ Fabric may shrink
- ☒ May bleed or fade

Where to find
- ☐ Any fabric store
- ☒ Major chain store
- ☒ Stores that carry high quality fabric
- ☒ Fabric club
- ☒ Mail order
- ☒ Wholesale supplier

ATTACH SAMPLE HERE

LENGTHWISE GRAIN

Douppioni has slubs and crosswise ribs.

douppioni

An elegant fabric woven with slubbed yarns of douppioni silk. This type of silk is used in a number of fabrics, but the classic douppioni cloth is made with a tight plain weave, fine warp yarns and heavier, slubbed filling yarns that form prominent, irregular crosswise ribs. Fabric is light to medium in weight, with a crisp, scrunchy hand, a rough, uneven texture and a dull luster. It is usually dyed brilliant colors and is often irridescent or plaid, but it may also be natural in color or bleached white.

Slubbed yarns

The irregular, crosswise ribs of douppioni are formed by filling yarns that have occasional soft, thick lumps. The lumps, or slubs, add texture and visual interest to the fabric, but they should be viewed with caution — the yarns are not very durable and tend to unravel. Fabrics tend to pill, pull apart at the seams and are subject to abrasion. Slubbed yarns are rarely used in the lengthwise direction because they are not strong enough to survive the great tension placed on warp yarns during weaving.

How to use

Douppioni has a moderately crisp drape that falls into wide cones. It can be lightly gathered into a lofty fullness, but too much fabric creates bulk. Fabric is sturdy and substantial, but not very durable: It scuffs easily and tends to pill. Crosswise yarns fray and ravel badly. Fabric is subject to seam slippage, so it is wise to avoid close-fitting styles that put stress on seams. Choose semi-fitted or loose-fitting styles to make blouses, dresses, skirts and lightweight suits. Should be drycleaned to avoid shrinkage and abrasions.

---

choked cocoon
A cocoon that is not finished because the silkworm has died. The silk is fine, but not as strong or brilliant as normal cocoons. It must be reeled separately because the silk often becomes tangled during the process. Also called cocoon chique, which is French for choked cocoon.

cocoon foible
A weak cocoon, larger and not as compact as a normal cocoon. It is reeled separately, immersed in colder water to avoid tangling.

cocoon pointus
A cocoon with a pointed end, producing a filament that usually breaks during reeling.

dragles
A British term for a cocoon in which the silkworm has died of muscardine, a disease that either hardens the cocoon or reduces it to a white powder. The cocoon produces an excellent quality silk in greater quantity than that of a healthy silkworm, but it is fairly rare.

Sewing rating
- [ ] Easy to sew
- [ ] Moderately easy
- [x] Average
- [ ] Moderately difficult
- [ ] Extremely difficult

Suggested fit
- [ ] Stretch to fit
- [ ] Close-fitting
- [ ] Fitted
- [x] Semi-fitted
- [x] Loose-fitting
- [ ] Very loose-fitting

Suggested styles
- [ ] Pleats [ ] Tucks
  - [ ] pressed
  - [ ] unpressed
- [x] Gathers
  - [ ] limp [ ] soft
  - [x] full [x] lofty
  - [ ] bouffant
- [ ] Elasticized shirring
- [ ] Smocked
- [x] Tailored
- [x] Shaped with seams to eliminate bulk
- [x] Lined
- [ ] Unlined
- [x] Puffed or bouffant
- [ ] Loose and full
- [ ] Soft and flowing
- [ ] Draped
- [ ] Cut on bias
- [ ] Stretch styling

What to expect
- [ ] Fabric is slippery, difficult to control
- [x] It is easy to cut out
- [ ] Difficult to cut out
- [ ] Fabric has a nap
- [x] Fabric is reversible
- [x] Both sides of fabric look the same
- [ ] It stretches easily
- [x] It will not stretch
- [x] It is difficult to ease sleeves and curves
- [ ] Fabric tears easily
- [ ] It is difficult to tear
- [ ] Fabric will not tear
- [x] Pins and needles leave holes, marks
- [ ] It tends to pucker
- [x] It tends to unravel
- [ ] Fabric won't unravel
- [ ] Inner construction shows from outside
- [ ] Machine eats fabric
- [ ] Skipped stitches
- [ ] Layers feed unevenly
- [ ] It creases easily
- [x] Won't hold a crease

Cost per yard
- [ ] Less than $10
- [x] $10 to $20
- [x] $20 to $30
- [ ] $30 to $40
- [ ] $40 to $50
- [ ] More than $50

Douppioni silk
Douppioni silk (meaning double) is produced when two or more silkworms spin their cocoons too close together. These slightly tangled cocoons produce filament that is rough, uneven and not as strong as cultivated silk. It is usually reeled and used to make fine or heavy yarns with pronounced irregular slubs at random intervals. Douppioni silk usually comes from cultivated, rather than wild, silkworms because their living quarters are more crowded, increasing their chances of tangling the cocoons. Like cultivated silk, douppioni is easy to dye, so fabrics are often brightly colored. The silk is used to make douppioni and shantung fabrics.

Wearability
- [ ] Durable [ ] Fragile
- [ ] Strong [ ] Weak
- [ ] It is long-wearing
- [ ] It wears evenly
- [ ] It wears out along seams and folds
- [x] Seams don't hold up under stress
- [x] Fabric is subject to abrasion
- [ ] It resists abrasion
- [ ] Subject to snags
- [ ] It resists snags
- [ ] Subject to runs
- [x] It tends to pill
- [ ] It tends to shed
- [ ] It attracts lint
- [ ] It attracts static
- [ ] It is static-free
- [ ] It tends to cling
- [x] It holds its shape
- [ ] It loses its shape
- [ ] It stretches out of shape easily
- [ ] It droops, bags
- [ ] It tends to wrinkle
- [x] It resists wrinkles
- [ ] It crushes easily
- [x] Water drops leave spots or marks

Suggested care
- [x] Dryclean only
- [ ] Do not dryclean
- [ ] Dryclean or wash
- [ ] Gently handwash in lukewarm water
- [ ] Roll in a towel to remove moisture
- [ ] Drip dry
- [ ] Lay flat to dry
- [ ] Machine wash
  - [ ] gentle/delicate
  - [ ] regular/normal
  - [ ] do not spin
- [ ] Machine dry
  - [ ] cool [ ] normal
  - [ ] perm. press
- [ ] Press damp fabric
- [x] Press dry fabric
- [x] Dry iron [ ] Steam
- [x] Iron on wrong side
- [ ] Use a press cloth
- [ ] Use a needleboard
- [ ] Needs no ironing
- [ ] Do not iron
- [x] Fabric may shrink
- [x] May bleed or fade

Where to find
- [ ] Any fabric store
- [x] Major chain store
- [x] Stores that carry high quality fabric
- [ ] Fabric club
- [x] Mail order
- [x] Wholesale supplier

ATTACH SAMPLE HERE

LENGTHWISE GRAIN

Four-ply silk is smooth and lustrous.

four-ply silk

Deluxe fabric with a sumptuous weight – it is obviously an expensive fabric. Four-ply silk is made with, you guessed it, four-ply yarns in both the warp and filling. Ply yarns are thicker, heavier, smoother, stronger and more uniform than single yarns, so fabric is thicker, stronger, smoother and more uniform as well. The weight varies from about 30mm to 40mm. Fabric looks the same on both sides and is very smooth and lustrous. It is usually available in whites and solid colors. Thailand and Korea are known for their four-ply silks, but these beautiful fabrics also are made in other countries.

How to use

Four-ply silk has an elegant drape that falls in fluid folds and flares. It can be gathered a bit, but too much fabric creates bulk. It won't hold a crease, so pleated styles should be avoided. Four-ply silk tailors beautifully and works well with styles that are shaped with seams. Use it to make elegant tailored suits, dresses, skirts, trousers, wedding gowns and evening wear.

Pure silk

"Pure silk" and "pure dyed silk" are terms used to describe top quality, all-silk fabrics that do not contain metallic weighting, a once-common practice used to disguise inferior quality silk. Weighting was added to the dyebath, hence the term "pure dyed." By law, pure silk and pure dyed silk may contain other finishing materials to give body to the fabric, such as starch or sizing, but this amount includes the dye and may not exceed 10 percent of the total weight of the fabric (15 percent for black.)

---

faille
Elegant, expensive fabric with a beautiful drape. It is made with a plain weave, fine warp yarns and slightly heavier filling yarns that form very fine, flat crosswise ribs on both sides. Faille (pronounced "file") is light to medium in weight, with a firm, soft, supple hand and a slightly grainy texture.

four-ply crepe
This term is used interchangeably with four-ply silk, but it also refers to silk crepe made with four-ply crepe yarns in one or both directions of the weave. It is not as smooth or lustrous as four-ply silk, but otherwise quite similar in weight, hand and cost.

three-ply silk
Expensive silk fabric made with three-ply yarns. Similar to four-ply silk, but lighter in weight. Also called three-ply crepe.

tissue faille
A very fine, thin version of faille that is usually quite lustrous, sometimes glossy.

Sewing rating
- ☐ Easy to sew
- ☐ Moderately easy
- ☐ Average
- ☒ Moderately difficult
- ☐ Extremely difficult

Suggested fit
- ☐ Stretch to fit
- ☐ Close-fitting
- ☒ Fitted
- ☒ Semi-fitted
- ☒ Loose-fitting
- ☐ Very loose-fitting

Suggested styles
- ☐ Pleats ☐ Tucks
  - ☐ pressed
  - ☐ unpressed
- ☒ Gathers
  - ☐ limp ☒ soft
  - ☐ full ☐ lofty
  - ☐ bouffant
- ☐ Elasticized shirring
- ☐ Smocked
- ☒ Tailored
- ☒ Shaped with seams to eliminate bulk
- ☐ Lined
- ☐ Unlined
- ☐ Puffed or bouffant
- ☒ Loose and full
- ☒ Soft and flowing
- ☒ Draped
- ☐ Cut on bias
- ☐ Stretch styling

What to expect
- ☒ Fabric is slippery, difficult to control
- ☐ It is easy to cut out
- ☒ Difficult to cut out
- ☐ Fabric has a nap
- ☐ Fabric is reversible
- ☒ Both sides of fabric look the same
- ☐ It stretches easily
- ☐ It will not stretch
- ☐ It is difficult to ease sleeves and curves
- ☒ Fabric tears easily
- ☐ It is difficult to tear
- ☐ Fabric will not tear
- ☐ Pins and needles leave holes, marks
- ☐ It tends to pucker
- ☐ It tends to unravel
- ☒ Fabric won't unravel
- ☐ Inner construction shows from outside
- ☐ Machine eats fabric
- ☐ Skipped stitches
- ☒ Layers feed unevenly
- ☐ It creases easily
- ☒ Won't hold a crease

Cost per yard
- ☐ Less than $10
- ☐ $10 to $20
- ☐ $20 to $30
- ☒ $30 to $40
- ☒ $40 to $50
- ☐ More than $50

How does a fabric drape?
Four-ply silk is cherished for its beautiful, graceful drape, the way it falls, hangs, clings, shapes, molds, pleats, gathers or flows on the body. All fabrics drape, but each one drapes or hangs differently. Factors that affect a fabric's drape include fiber content, type of yarn, type of weave and type of finish, if any, applied to fibers, yarns or the fabric. Fabrics that appear to be similar may drape in dramatically different ways. A twill fabric, for example, will drape differently than a rib fabric made from the same fiber and type of yarn, as will a similar fabric finished with sizing or starch.

Wearability
- ☒ Durable ☐ Fragile
- ☒ Strong ☐ Weak
- ☒ It is long-wearing
- ☒ It wears evenly
- ☐ It wears out along seams and folds
- ☐ Seams don't hold up under stress
- ☒ Fabric is subject to abrasion
- ☐ It resists abrasion
- ☐ Subject to snags
- ☐ It resists snags
- ☐ Subject to runs
- ☐ It tends to pill

- ☐ It tends to shed
- ☐ It attracts lint
- ☐ It attracts static
- ☐ It is static-free
- ☐ It tends to cling
- ☒ It holds its shape
- ☐ It loses its shape
- ☐ It stretches out of shape easily
- ☐ It droops, bags
- ☐ It tends to wrinkle
- ☒ It resists wrinkles
- ☐ It crushes easily
- ☐ Water drops leave spots or marks

Suggested care
- ☐ Dryclean only
- ☐ Do not dryclean
- ☒ Dryclean or wash
- ☒ Gently handwash in lukewarm water
- ☒ Roll in a towel to remove moisture
- ☐ Drip dry
- ☒ Lay flat to dry
- ☐ Machine wash
  - ☐ gentle/delicate
  - ☐ regular/normal
  - ☐ do not spin
- ☐ Machine dry
  - ☐ cool ☐ normal
  - ☐ perm. press
- ☒ Press damp fabric
- ☐ Press dry fabric
- ☒ Dry iron ☐ Steam
- ☐ Iron on wrong side
- ☒ Use a press cloth
- ☐ Use a needleboard
- ☐ Needs no ironing
- ☐ Do not iron
- ☒ Fabric may shrink
- ☒ May bleed or fade

Where to find
- ☐ Any fabric store
- ☐ Major chain store
- ☒ Stores that carry high quality fabric
- ☐ Fabric club
- ☒ Mail order
- ☒ Wholesale supplier

ATTACH SAMPLE HERE

LENGTHWISE GRAIN

Silk gabardine has a very dry hand.

gabardine

A dressy, firmly woven twill fabric with a fine, indistinct diagonal line on one or both sides – it is sometimes a true gabardine and sometimes not. The fabric is typically very flat, almost smooth, with a springy, very dry hand and a hint of luster dulled by the tight weave. The weight varies, but it is usually more substantial than other silk twills. This uncommon fabric is usually available in only a few neutral and basic colors. Some versions are made of silk blended with other fibers.

True gabardine
Gabardine is a type of twill with specific characteristics. The fabric has a distinct, closely set, raised diagonal line on the right side and a smooth, plain back. Fabric with a visible twill line on both sides is not true gabardine. The diagonal twill line may run in either direction, but the angle of the twill is usually 45 or 63 degrees. The word "gabardine" originally was used to describe a cloak worn in the Middle Ages. Today, the fabric is typically made of worsted wool and used to make suits.

How to use

Silk gabardine has a beautiful drape that falls close to the body and tends to cling. It may be gathered into a moderately lofty fullness. The fabric resists wrinkles, but with a little effort, it may be pleated into crisp, pressed folds. Armholes and other curved seams are difficult to ease and may pucker. Like all gabardines, fabric is durable, but it shows wear along folds and hem lines and tends to unravel. Choose fitted or semi-fitted styles to make slacks, skirts and lightweight suits. Dryclean or handwash, but beware of shrinkage.

---

satin gabardine
Gabardine with long satin floats on the face of the fabric. May be silk or wool.

sheer gabardine
An open-weave gabardine, often made of silk, showing the filling. Used chiefly for dresses. Also called voile gabardine.

serge
A clear-finished fabric with a flat twill line that runs from the lower left to the upper right, made with a two-up, two-down twill. Originally made of silk, now usually made of worsted wool or cotton. Today's silk serge is a much lighter fabric that is more often called surah or silk twill.

even twill
Any twill fabric with the same number of warp yarns above and below the filling yarns. For example, a two-up, two-down twill has two warp yarns that pass over one filling yarn; the next two warp yarns pass under the same filling yarn. Also called a balanced twill.

Sewing rating
- [ ] Easy to sew
- [x] Moderately easy
- [ ] Average
- [ ] Moderately difficult
- [ ] Extremely difficult

Suggested fit
- [ ] Stretch to fit
- [ ] Close-fitting
- [x] Fitted
- [x] Semi-fitted
- [ ] Loose-fitting
- [ ] Very loose-fitting

Suggested styles
- [x] Pleats [ ] Tucks
  - [x] pressed
  - [ ] unpressed
- [x] Gathers
  - [ ] limp [ ] soft
  - [x] full [ ] lofty
  - [ ] bouffant
- [ ] Elasticized shirring
- [ ] Smocked
- [x] Tailored
- [x] Shaped with seams to eliminate bulk
- [x] Lined
- [ ] Unlined
- [ ] Puffed or bouffant
- [ ] Loose and full
- [ ] Soft and flowing
- [x] Draped
- [ ] Cut on bias
- [ ] Stretch styling

What to expect
- [ ] Fabric is slippery, difficult to control
- [x] It is easy to cut out
- [ ] Difficult to cut out
- [x] Fabric has a nap
- [ ] Fabric is reversible
- [ ] Both sides of fabric look the same
- [ ] It stretches easily
- [ ] It will not stretch
- [x] It is difficult to ease sleeves and curves
- [ ] Fabric tears easily
- [ ] It is difficult to tear
- [x] Fabric will not tear
- [ ] Pins and needles leave holes, marks
- [x] It tends to pucker
- [x] It tends to unravel
- [ ] Fabric won't unravel
- [ ] Inner construction shows from outside
- [ ] Machine eats fabric
- [ ] Skipped stitches
- [ ] Layers feed unevenly
- [ ] It creases easily
- [ ] Won't hold a crease

Cost per yard
- [ ] Less than $10
- [ ] $10 to $20
- [x] $20 to $30
- [ ] $30 to $40
- [ ] $40 to $50
- [ ] More than $50

The twill weave
Twill is the strongest and most durable of the basic weaves. It is easily recognised by a diagonal rib, or twill line, on one or both sides of the fabric. A typical weave pattern has warp yarns that float over or under at least two consecutive filling yarns. On each row, the filling yarn shifts over one warp yarn, creating the twill line. The pattern can be varied in many ways, creating a steep, reclining, broken or zigzag line. Many twill fabrics shrink and fray badly, and they tend to wear out along edges and folds. Gabardine and denim are good examples of twill fabric.

Wearability
- [x] Durable [ ] Fragile
- [x] Strong [ ] Weak
- [ ] It is long-wearing
- [ ] It wears evenly
- [x] It wears out along seams and folds
- [ ] Seams don't hold up under stress
- [ ] Fabric is subject to abrasion
- [ ] It resists abrasion
- [ ] Subject to snags
- [ ] It resists snags
- [ ] Subject to runs
- [ ] It tends to pill
- [ ] It tends to shed
- [ ] It attracts lint
- [ ] It attracts static
- [ ] It is static-free
- [x] It tends to cling
- [ ] It holds its shape
- [ ] It loses its shape
- [ ] It stretches out of shape easily
- [ ] It droops, bags
- [ ] It tends to wrinkle
- [x] It resists wrinkles
- [ ] It crushes easily
- [ ] Water drops leave spots or marks

Suggested care
- [ ] Dryclean only
- [ ] Do not dryclean
- [x] Dryclean or wash
- [x] Gently handwash in lukewarm water
- [x] Roll in a towel to remove moisture
- [x] Drip dry
- [ ] Lay flat to dry
- [ ] Machine wash
  - [ ] gentle/delicate
  - [ ] regular/normal
  - [ ] do not spin
- [ ] Machine dry
  - [ ] cool [ ] normal
  - [ ] perm. press
- [x] Press damp fabric
- [ ] Press dry fabric
- [x] Dry iron [ ] Steam
- [x] Iron on wrong side
- [x] Use a press cloth
- [ ] Use a needleboard
- [ ] Needs no ironing
- [ ] Do not iron
- [x] Fabric may shrink
- [ ] May bleed or fade

Where to find
- [ ] Any fabric store
- [ ] Major chain store
- [x] Stores that carry high quality fabric
- [ ] Fabric club
- [x] Mail order
- [x] Wholesale supplier

ATTACH SAMPLE HERE

LENGTHWISE GRAIN

Georgette is not as soft as chiffon.

georgette

A harsh crepe fabric named after Madame Georgette de la Plante, a French milliner. It is made with alternating S- and Z-twist crepe yarns in both directions of a loose plain weave. Fabric has a grainy, sheer texture and a thin, very dry hand. The term is often used interchangeably with chiffon, but georgette is not as soft, has less luster and more crepe. Fabric is usually made with ply yarns and is often dyed or printed. It is sometimes woven of raw silk and then degummed, producing a crepe finish. There are many synthetic versions.

How to use

Silk georgette drapes beautifully and falls into soft, languid flares and ripples. It may be gathered, shirred or pleated into a limp fullness. Seams, facings and interfacings can be seen from the finished side of the garment. Fabric is durable, but it snags easily and is extremely difficult to sew. Choose loose, full styles to make blouses, bias-cut, flared skirts and dresses, evening wear and scarves. Dryclean only.

Sheer agony

Lightweight, sheer fabrics like silk chiffon and georgette are extremely difficult to cut and sew. These fabrics are slippery, snag easily and tend to pucker. But by far the most irritating, damaging problem is the machine's constant effort to swallow the fabric through the hole in the throatplate. It helps to use a fine (size 8), sharp needle, small, straight stitches and a throatplate with a very small hole. One solution is to cover the hole with a piece of masking tape or scotch tape.

---

crepe Elizabeth
A British term for a georgette fabric with a pebbled or mottled appearance that is very pronounced.

crepe georgette
Another name for georgette. The term is redundant because georgette is crepe.

double georgette
A heavier version of georgette, made with two-ply yarns. Has more weight and body.

georgine
A very light, fine fabric similar to georgette, woven of partially degummed silk. The rest of the gum is removed after weaving.

satin georgette
A heavy sheer fabric made of tightly twisted yarns in a satin weave, introduced in about 1930. Used for evening wear.

triple georgette
A heavier version of georgette, made with three-ply yarns.

Sewing rating
- ☐ Easy to sew
- ☐ Moderately easy
- ☐ Average
- ☐ Moderately difficult
- ☒ Extremely difficult

Suggested fit
- ☐ Stretch to fit
- ☐ Close-fitting
- ☐ Fitted
- ☒ Semi-fitted
- ☒ Loose-fitting
- ☒ Very loose-fitting

Suggested styles
- ☐ Pleats ☒ Tucks
  - ☐ pressed
  - ☒ unpressed
- ☒ Gathers
  - ☒ limp ☐ soft
  - ☐ full ☐ lofty
  - ☐ bouffant
- ☒ Elasticized shirring
- ☐ Smocked
- ☐ Tailored
- ☐ Shaped with seams to eliminate bulk
- ☒ Lined
- ☐ Unlined
- ☐ Puffed or bouffant
- ☒ Loose and full
- ☒ Soft and flowing
- ☒ Draped
- ☒ Cut on bias
- ☐ Stretch styling

What to expect
- ☒ Fabric is slippery, difficult to control
- ☐ It is easy to cut out
- ☒ Difficult to cut out
- ☐ Fabric has a nap
- ☒ Fabric is reversible
- ☒ Both sides of fabric look the same
- ☐ It stretches easily
- ☐ It will not stretch
- ☐ It is difficult to ease sleeves and curves
- ☒ Fabric tears easily
- ☐ It is difficult to tear
- ☐ Fabric will not tear
- ☐ Pins and needles leave holes, marks
- ☒ It tends to pucker
- ☐ It tends to unravel
- ☐ Fabric won't unravel
- ☒ Inner construction shows from outside
- ☒ Machine eats fabric
- ☐ Skipped stitches
- ☐ Layers feed unevenly
- ☐ It creases easily
- ☒ Won't hold a crease

Cost per yard
- ☐ Less than $10
- ☐ $10 to $20
- ☒ $20 to $30
- ☒ $30 to $40
- ☒ $40 to $50
- ☐ More than $50

Ply yarns

Georgette is usually woven with two-ply or three-ply yarns, made by twisting together two or three single strands. A two-ply yarn has two individual strands, a three-ply yarn has three, and so forth. When a ply yarn is untwisted, the single strands can be counted. When a single yarn is untwisted, the fibers separate and come apart. Ply yarns are thicker, heavier, smoother, stronger and more uniform than single yarns. Single yarns are more flexible. A yarn's ply affects the fabric's characteristics, including weight, texture and drape. That is why chiffon, made from singles, is usually softer and more delicate than georgette.

Wearability
- ☒ Durable ☐ Fragile
- ☒ Strong ☐ Weak
- ☒ It is long-wearing
- ☒ It wears evenly
- ☐ It wears out along seams and folds
- ☐ Seams don't hold up under stress
- ☐ Fabric is subject to abrasion
- ☐ It resists abrasion
- ☒ Subject to snags
- ☐ It resists snags
- ☐ Subject to runs
- ☐ It tends to pill
- ☐ It tends to shed
- ☐ It attracts lint
- ☐ It attracts static
- ☐ It is static-free
- ☐ It tends to cling
- ☐ It holds its shape
- ☐ It loses its shape
- ☐ It stretches out of shape easily
- ☐ It droops, bags
- ☐ It tends to wrinkle
- ☒ It resists wrinkles
- ☐ It crushes easily
- ☒ Water drops leave spots or marks

Suggested care
- ☒ Dryclean only
- ☐ Do not dryclean
- ☐ Dryclean or wash
- ☐ Gently handwash in lukewarm water
- ☐ Roll in a towel to remove moisture
- ☐ Drip dry
- ☐ Lay flat to dry
- ☐ Machine wash
  - ☐ gentle/delicate
  - ☐ regular/normal
  - ☐ do not spin
- ☐ Machine dry
  - ☐ cool ☐ normal
  - ☐ perm. press
- ☐ Press damp fabric
- ☒ Press dry fabric
- ☒ Dry iron ☐ Steam
- ☐ Iron on wrong side
- ☐ Use a press cloth
- ☐ Use a needleboard
- ☐ Needs no ironing
- ☐ Do not iron
- ☒ Fabric may shrink
- ☐ May bleed or fade

Where to find
- ☐ Any fabric store
- ☐ Major chain store
- ☒ Stores that carry high quality fabric
- ☐ Fabric club
- ☒ Mail order
- ☒ Wholesale supplier

Habutai is smooth, limp and very soft.

habutai

Means "soft as down" in Japanese. A soft, fine to lightweight silk made with a plain or twill weave and slightly twisted yarns. It was originally handwoven of single warp yarns and filling yarns of hand-reeled silk, which made it slightly irregular. Habutai is usually a natural, ecru color, although it is sometimes bleached white or dyed. Fabric has a smooth, thin, limp hand. It varies in weight from 5mm to 10mm or more; 8mm is common. Habutai is often called China silk, but authentic habutai is slightly heavier, slightly irregular and has more luster than China silk. It is also spelled habutae, habotai and hautae.

How to use

Habutai has a soft, graceful drape that falls close to the body and may be gathered or shirred into a limp fullness. Fabric is moderately easy to cut and sew, but requires a gentle touch. Choose semi-fitted, loose-fitting or very loose-fitting styles of dresses and blouses. Heavier versions are sometimes used to make very lightweight jackets. Dryclean or gently handwash.

Mm = momme

Some silk fabric labels include a numerical measure, such as 8mm habutai or 4mm chiffon. The "mm" stands for momme, a Japanese unit of weight used by the textile industry as the standard way to measure and describe silk fabrics. A momme equals 3.75 grams. The higher the momme, the heavier the fabric. Most fabrics are made in several weights. For example, 10mm habutai is heavier than 5mm habutai. Momme is also spelled momie or mommie, but it sounds like mummy.

---

fukui habutai

The heaviest grade of Japanese habutai.

geisha silk

Trade name for a type of dyed habutai. The term is also used in France for a very fine gauze fabric made with an unusual weave, similar to a thin voile or veiling.

habutai de Suisse

A trade name for a low-luster, pure-dye silk fabric that resembles habutai.

kimono silk

Soft, plain-weave fabric used in Japan for kimonos and linings. Slightly heavier than habutai, printed with elaborate designs.

laundered habutai

Habutai treated to an abrasive wash to create a softly wrinkled, easy-care fabric that can be machine washed and dried and needs no ironing.

shusu-habutai

Habutai made with a satin weave.

Sewing rating
- [ ] Easy to sew
- [x] Moderately easy
- [ ] Average
- [ ] Moderately difficult
- [ ] Extremely difficult

Suggested fit
- [ ] Stretch to fit
- [ ] Close-fitting
- [ ] Fitted
- [x] Semi-fitted
- [x] Loose-fitting
- [x] Very loose-fitting

Suggested styles
- [ ] Pleats [ ] Tucks
  - [ ] pressed
  - [ ] unpressed
- [x] Gathers
  - [x] limp [x] soft
  - [ ] full [ ] lofty
  - [ ] bouffant
- [x] Elasticized shirring
- [ ] Smocked
- [ ] Tailored
- [ ] Shaped with seams to eliminate bulk
- [ ] Lined
- [ ] Unlined
- [ ] Puffed or bouffant
- [x] Loose and full
- [x] Soft and flowing
- [x] Draped
- [ ] Cut on bias
- [ ] Stretch styling

What to expect
- [ ] Fabric is slippery, difficult to control
- [ ] It is easy to cut out
- [ ] Difficult to cut out
- [ ] Fabric has a nap
- [x] Fabric is reversible
- [x] Both sides of fabric look the same
- [ ] It stretches easily
- [ ] It will not stretch
- [ ] It is difficult to ease sleeves and curves
- [x] Fabric tears easily
- [ ] It is difficult to tear
- [ ] Fabric will not tear
- [ ] Pins and needles leave holes, marks
- [ ] It tends to pucker
- [ ] It tends to unravel
- [ ] Fabric won't unravel
- [ ] Inner construction shows from outside
- [ ] Machine eats fabric
- [ ] Skipped stitches
- [ ] Layers feed unevenly
- [x] It creases easily
- [ ] Won't hold a crease

Cost per yard
- [x] Less than $10
- [x] $10 to $20
- [x] $20 to $30
- [ ] $30 to $40
- [ ] $40 to $50
- [ ] More than $50

Silk from Japan
Japan's silk industry dates back to about 200 A.D., when a gift of silkworm eggs was received from China's emperor, at a time when sericulture was a closely guarded secret. This was followed by the arrival of an exiled Chinese prince, whose entourage included skilled silk weavers. For several centuries, Japan's silk industry rivaled China's, but China gave in to European influence and its fabrics changed. Japan began to develop elaborate printing and dyeing techniques, and was the first country to take a scientific approach to sericulture. Today, Japan is known for its high quality silk and exquisite prints. Japan produces 20 percent of the world's silk.

Wearability
- [ ] Durable [ ] Fragile
- [ ] Strong [ ] Weak
- [ ] It is long-wearing
- [x] It wears evenly
- [ ] It wears out along seams and folds
- [ ] Seams don't hold up under stress
- [ ] Fabric is subject to abrasion
- [ ] It resists abrasion
- [ ] Subject to snags
- [x] It resists snags
- [ ] Subject to runs
- [ ] It tends to pill

- [ ] It tends to shed
- [ ] It attracts lint
- [ ] It attracts static
- [ ] It is static-free
- [ ] It tends to cling
- [ ] It holds its shape
- [ ] It loses its shape
- [ ] It stretches out of shape easily
- [ ] It droops, bags
- [x] It tends to wrinkle
- [ ] It resists wrinkles
- [ ] It crushes easily
- [ ] Water drops leave spots or marks

Suggested care
- [ ] Dryclean only
- [ ] Do not dryclean
- [x] Dryclean or wash
- [x] Gently handwash in lukewarm water
- [x] Roll in a towel to remove moisture
- [x] Drip dry
- [ ] Lay flat to dry
- [ ] Machine wash
  - [ ] gentle/delicate
  - [ ] regular/normal
  - [ ] do not spin
- [ ] Machine dry
  - [ ] cool [ ] normal
  - [ ] perm. press
- [x] Press damp fabric
- [ ] Press dry fabric
- [x] Dry iron [ ] Steam
- [ ] Iron on wrong side
- [ ] Use a press cloth
- [ ] Use a needleboard
- [ ] Needs no ironing
- [ ] Do not iron
- [ ] Fabric may shrink
- [ ] May bleed or fade

Where to find
- [ ] Any fabric store
- [ ] Major chain store
- [x] Stores that carry high quality fabric
- [ ] Fabric club
- [x] Mail order
- [x] Wholesale supplier

ATTACH SAMPLE HERE

LENGTHWISE GRAIN

Jacquard has a lustrous-and-dull pattern.

jacquard

This smooth, elegant fabric, made on a jacquard loom, has a complex woven design. The warp yarns usually form satin floats that dominate one side, while the fillings produce a predominately crepe or twill effect on the other. The satin-and-crepe combination is used to form a lustrous-and-dull pattern that reverses itself on the flip side. The side with the prominent warp yarns is generally considered to be the face, but either side may be used. The weight varies and fabric has a soft, limp or slightly crisp hand, depending on the weave. It is sometimes overprinted with a contrasting color, negating its reversibility.

How to use

Silk jacquard has a soft, graceful drape that falls close to the body and may cling, depending on the weave. Fabric may be gathered or shirred into a soft fullness. Crisper versions may be pleated. Choose loose, flowing, draped or flared styles for blouses, dresses, evening wear and lingerie. Dryclean to avoid snags and scuffs. Sandwashed versions can be machine washed and dried.

Static cling

Silk fiber does not collect much static, and thus, is not likely to cling. But fiber content is not the only contributor to static. The type of weave, yarn and/or finish also affect a fabric's tendency to cling. Charmeuse and jacquard cling more than other silk fabrics, but less than their synthetic counterparts. When silk clings, it is usually because the fiber has become too dry. This is easy to fix: Simply hang the garment in a steamy bathroom so it can absorb a little moisture.

---

crepe jacquard
A term sometimes given to fabrics with jacquard figures on a crepe background.

damask satin
A very lustrous damask fabric with both the background and pattern formed by satin weaves, made on a jacquard loom.

donsu
A Japanese silk damask. Murasakiji-donsu is a violet-colored damask used for drapes.

hammered silk
A shimmery silk dress fabric with a pattern that looks like hammered metal, made on a jacquard loom.

silk damask
A more accurate name for silk jacquard. Technically, damask is a type of fabric and jacquard is the loom used to make it. But the distinction between the two terms has blurred, and today, many fabrics woven on a jacquard loom are simply called jacquard, including heavy brocades and tapestries.

Sewing rating
- [ ] Easy to sew
- [ ] Moderately easy
- [x] Average
- [ ] Moderately difficult
- [ ] Extremely difficult

Suggested fit
- [ ] Stretch to fit
- [ ] Close-fitting
- [ ] Fitted
- [x] Semi-fitted
- [x] Loose-fitting
- [x] Very loose-fitting

Suggested styles
- [x] Pleats [x] Tucks
  - [ ] pressed
  - [x] unpressed
- [x] Gathers
  - [ ] limp [x] soft
  - [x] full [ ] lofty
  - [ ] bouffant
- [x] Elasticized shirring
- [ ] Smocked
- [ ] Tailored
- [ ] Shaped with seams to eliminate bulk
- [ ] Lined
- [ ] Unlined
- [ ] Puffed or bouffant
- [x] Loose and full
- [x] Soft and flowing
- [x] Draped
- [x] Cut on bias
- [ ] Stretch styling

What to expect
- [x] Fabric is slippery, difficult to control
- [ ] It is easy to cut out
- [x] Difficult to cut out
- [ ] Fabric has a nap
- [x] Fabric is reversible
- [ ] Both sides of fabric look the same
- [ ] It stretches easily
- [ ] It will not stretch
- [ ] It is difficult to ease sleeves and curves
- [ ] Fabric tears easily
- [ ] It is difficult to tear
- [x] Fabric will not tear
- [ ] Pins and needles leave holes, marks
- [ ] It tends to pucker
- [ ] It tends to unravel
- [ ] Fabric won't unravel
- [ ] Inner construction shows from outside
- [ ] Machine eats fabric
- [ ] Skipped stitches
- [ ] Layers feed unevenly
- [x] It creases easily
- [ ] Won't hold a crease

Cost per yard
- [ ] Less than $10
- [x] $10 to $20
- [x] $20 to $30
- [x] $30 to $40
- [ ] $40 to $50
- [ ] More than $50

Jacquard weave

The jacquard loom uses the three basic weaves – plain, twill and satin – to form complicated floral or figured patterns on a simpler background. The complex loom was developed in France during the early 1800s by Joseph-Marie Jacquard. The loom mechanized figure weaving, an expensive, time-consuming task done by hand. Today's computerized looms allow up to 1,200 yarns to have independent weave action, and are used to make woven and knit fabrics with intricate designs, including brocade, damask and tapestry. It is still an expensive form of weaving.

Wearability
- [ ] Durable [x] Fragile
- [ ] Strong [ ] Weak
- [ ] It is long-wearing
- [ ] It wears evenly
- [ ] It wears out along seams and folds
- [ ] Seams don't hold up under stress
- [x] Fabric is subject to abrasion
- [ ] It resists abrasion
- [x] Subject to snags
- [ ] It resists snags
- [ ] Subject to runs
- [ ] It tends to pill

- [ ] It tends to shed
- [ ] It attracts lint
- [x] It attracts static
- [ ] It is static-free
- [x] It tends to cling
- [ ] It holds its shape
- [ ] It loses its shape
- [ ] It stretches out of shape easily
- [ ] It droops, bags
- [x] It tends to wrinkle
- [ ] It resists wrinkles
- [ ] It crushes easily
- [x] Water drops leave spots or marks

Suggested care
- [ ] Dryclean only
- [ ] Do not dryclean
- [x] Dryclean or wash
- [x] Gently handwash in lukewarm water
- [x] Roll in a towel to remove moisture
- [x] Drip dry
- [ ] Lay flat to dry
- [ ] Machine wash
  - [ ] gentle/delicate
  - [ ] regular/normal
  - [ ] do not spin
- [ ] Machine dry
  - [ ] cool [ ] normal
  - [ ] perm. press
- [ ] Press damp fabric
- [x] Press dry fabric
- [x] Dry iron [ ] Steam
- [x] Iron on wrong side
- [x] Use a press cloth
- [ ] Use a needleboard
- [ ] Needs no ironing
- [ ] Do not iron
- [x] Fabric may shrink
- [x] May bleed or fade

Where to find
- [ ] Any fabric store
- [x] Major chain store
- [x] Stores that carry high quality fabric
- [x] Fabric club
- [x] Mail order
- [x] Wholesale supplier

ATTACH SAMPLE HERE

LENGTHWISE GRAIN

Silk knit is soft and dressy.

knit

Very expensive, soft, dressy fabrics that are warm and comfortable to wear. One of the most common knits is a lightweight double knit that resembles cotton interlock in thickness and weight, especially when made of spun silk yarns. The fabric usually has fine lengthwise ribs on both sides, and when well-made, it is run-resistant. Silk knits are not as warm as wool, but they are warmer than cotton versions and more luxurious. Fabrics are usually available in underwear colors – black, white, pale pink, natural – although fashion colors are becoming more common and some versions are printed.

How to use

Silk knit has a beautiful drape that falls close to the body in soft, fluid ripples and tends to cling. Fabrics are difficult to cut and sew because they are quite slippery and prone to stretching, especially in the crosswise direction. Use to make pullover tops, skirts, dresses and long underwear. Shrinkage is common; drycleaning is recommended unless the fabric has been preshrunk.

Silk 'woolies'

Silk garments are warm and toasty in cold weather because silk is a low conductor of heat, meaning the fiber traps heat and is slow to release it. Silk is comfortable in hot and cold weather because it is porous, allowing the skin to breathe freely. Silk absorbs moisture easily, so it wicks perspiration away from the body. Wool is the warmest, most absorbent natural fiber, but wool itches when worn next to the skin. Silk, which does not itch, is perfect for long underwear.

---

double knit

Also called double jersey. Medium to heavy fabric knitted with two sets of needles, so that both sides look the same. The fabric has little or no stretch in either direction and holds its shape well. Silk double knit is not as heavy as cotton and wool versions and tends to stretch more.

interlock

A closely knit fabric with flat indistinct ribs on both sides, usually made of cotton or a cotton/polyester blend. Fabric is flat and smooth, with a controlled stretch in the crosswise direction. Interlock is usually thicker and heavier than its cousin, jersey. It lies flat and does not curl at the edges.

jersey

A lightweight, smooth single-knit fabric with flat indistinct ribs on the front and a plain back, usually made of wool, cotton or a cotton/polyester blend. Jersey has an easy crosswise stretch, but only a slight lengthwise stretch, and it tends to curl at the edges. Silk jersey is especially thin.

Sewing rating
- ☐ Easy to sew
- ☐ Moderately easy
- ☐ Average
- ☒ Moderately difficult
- ☐ Extremely difficult

Suggested fit
- ☒ Stretch to fit
- ☒ Close-fitting
- ☐ Fitted
- ☐ Semi-fitted
- ☒ Loose-fitting
- ☐ Very loose-fitting

Suggested styles
- ☐ Pleats ☐ Tucks
  - ☐ pressed
  - ☐ unpressed
- ☒ Gathers
  - ☐ limp ☒ soft
  - ☐ full ☐ lofty
  - ☐ bouffant
- ☒ Elasticized shirring
- ☐ Smocked
- ☐ Tailored
- ☐ Shaped with seams to eliminate bulk
- ☐ Lined
- ☐ Unlined
- ☐ Puffed or bouffant
- ☒ Loose and full
- ☒ Soft and flowing
- ☒ Draped
- ☐ Cut on bias
- ☒ Stretch styling

What to expect
- ☒ Fabric is slippery, difficult to control
- ☐ It is easy to cut out
- ☒ Difficult to cut out
- ☐ Fabric has a nap
- ☒ Fabric is reversible
- ☒ Both sides of fabric look the same
- ☒ It stretches easily
- ☐ It will not stretch
- ☐ It is difficult to ease sleeves and curves
- ☐ Fabric tears easily
- ☐ It is difficult to tear
- ☒ Fabric will not tear
- ☐ Pins and needles leave holes, marks
- ☐ It tends to pucker
- ☐ It tends to unravel
- ☐ Fabric won't unravel
- ☐ Inner construction shows from outside
- ☐ Machine eats fabric
- ☐ Skipped stitches
- ☐ Layers feed unevenly
- ☐ It creases easily
- ☒ Won't hold a crease

Cost per yard
- ☐ Less than $10
- ☐ $10 to $20
- ☐ $20 to $30
- ☒ $30 to $40
- ☒ $40 to $50
- ☐ More than $50

Knitting lingo
Knit fabrics are made by interlacing rows of loops together. The smallest unit in a knit is called a **stitch**, made by pulling a knitted loop through a previously formed loop. A lengthwise row of loops is called a **wale**. One loop in a wale is formed under another, using the same needle. A crosswise row of loops is called a **course**. Each loop in a course is formed next to another, using a different needle. A **single knit** is made on a machine with one set of needles, while a **double knit** requires two sets that work together to join two sets of loops. Yarns and stitches can be varied to achieve different effects.

Wearability
- ☐ Durable ☐ Fragile
- ☐ Strong ☐ Weak
- ☐ It is long-wearing
- ☒ It wears evenly
- ☐ It wears out along seams and folds
- ☐ Seams don't hold up under stress
- ☐ Fabric is subject to abrasion
- ☐ It resists abrasion
- ☒ Subject to snags
- ☐ It resists snags
- ☒ Subject to runs
- ☐ It tends to pill
- ☐ It tends to shed
- ☒ It attracts lint
- ☐ It attracts static
- ☐ It is static-free
- ☒ It tends to cling
- ☐ It holds its shape
- ☐ It loses its shape
- ☒ It stretches out of shape easily
- ☐ It droops, bags
- ☐ It tends to wrinkle
- ☒ It resists wrinkles
- ☐ It crushes easily
- ☐ Water drops leave spots or marks

Suggested care
- ☐ Dryclean only
- ☐ Do not dryclean
- ☒ Dryclean or wash
- ☒ Gently handwash in lukewarm water
- ☒ Roll in a towel to remove moisture
- ☐ Drip dry
- ☒ Lay flat to dry
- ☐ Machine wash
  - ☐ gentle/delicate
  - ☐ regular/normal
  - ☐ do not spin
- ☐ Machine dry
  - ☐ cool ☐ normal
  - ☐ perm. press
- ☐ Press damp fabric
- ☐ Press dry fabric
- ☐ Dry iron ☐ Steam
- ☐ Iron on wrong side
- ☐ Use a press cloth
- ☐ Use a needleboard
- ☒ Needs no ironing
- ☐ Do not iron
- ☒ Fabric may shrink
- ☐ May bleed or fade

Where to find
- ☐ Any fabric store
- ☐ Major chain store
- ☒ Stores that carry high quality fabric
- ☐ Fabric club
- ☒ Mail order
- ☒ Wholesale supplier

LENGTHWISE GRAIN

Silk matelassé has two distinct layers.

matelassé

French for "cushioned" or "padded." True matelassé is a type of double cloth, made by joining two distinct layers to produce a puffy, raised effect on the face. The original version, made of silk, was padded between the layers and quilted. Today's matelassé has shed the padding and is much lighter in weight. It is usually woven on a jacquard or dobby loom with two extra sets of crepe yarns. The layers are woven with different tensions and shrunk after weaving, causing one layer to tighten up and the other to puff up. There are many synthetic imitations, most of which are embossed.

How to use

Matelassé has a soft, spongy, springy hand. Its puffiness is exaggerated when the fabric is gathered. Otherwise, it will hold the shape of the garment. Choose semi-fitted or loose-fitting styles to make blouses, dresses, suits and evening wear. Fabric travels well and needs little or no ironing. Some versions can be machine washed and dried, but drycleaning is recommended.

Padding

Until the recent surge in silk's popularity, silk waste was rarely spun into yarn. Instead, it was made into wadding, used to pad or stuff upholstery and clothing. Wadding is obsolete, but another type of padding, called batting, is sometimes made of silk. This slightly matted sheet of fiber is most often used to pad quilts, and is usually made of cotton, wool or synthetic fibers. Silk batts have superior insulating qualities, but they are not very common or very big, usually 20 x 40 inches or 40 x 80 inches.

---

gaufré (gaffered silk)
An embossed effect produced by pressing the fabric between hot rollers, resulting in high-relief patterns such as honeycomb, waffle and crimp. Derived from the French word "gaufrer," meaning to figure fabric or velvet. A similar method is used to make cloqué and embossed matelassé.

piqué
A type of textured double cloth available with a variety of surface patterns, such as birdseye piqué, pigskin piqué, pinwale piqué and spiral piqué. Usually made of cotton, but rayon or silk is sometimes used. Silk piqué tends to be expensive because it is not very common.

soufflé
Term used to describe fabrics with raised or puffed designs. It is French for "puffed."

trapunto
Quilting technique that produces a padded design outlined with single stitches. Each section is filled in separately from the back.

Sewing rating
- [ ] Easy to sew
- [ ] Moderately easy
- [x] Average
- [ ] Moderately difficult
- [ ] Extremely difficult

Suggested fit
- [ ] Stretch to fit
- [ ] Close-fitting
- [ ] Fitted
- [x] Semi-fitted
- [x] Loose-fitting
- [ ] Very loose-fitting

Suggested styles
- [ ] Pleats [ ] Tucks
  - [ ] pressed
  - [ ] unpressed
- [x] Gathers
  - [ ] limp [ ] soft
  - [x] full [x] lofty
  - [ ] bouffant
- [ ] Elasticized shirring
- [ ] Smocked
- [ ] Tailored
- [x] Shaped with seams to eliminate bulk
- [x] Lined
- [ ] Unlined
- [x] Puffed or bouffant
- [x] Loose and full
- [ ] Soft and flowing
- [ ] Draped
- [ ] Cut on bias
- [ ] Stretch styling

What to expect
- [ ] Fabric is slippery, difficult to control
- [x] It is easy to cut out
- [ ] Difficult to cut out
- [ ] Fabric has a nap
- [ ] Fabric is reversible
- [ ] Both sides of fabric look the same
- [ ] It stretches easily
- [ ] It will not stretch
- [ ] It is difficult to ease sleeves and curves
- [ ] Fabric tears easily
- [ ] It is difficult to tear
- [x] Fabric will not tear
- [ ] Pins and needles leave holes, marks
- [ ] It tends to pucker
- [ ] It tends to unravel
- [x] Fabric won't unravel
- [ ] Inner construction shows from outside
- [ ] Machine eats fabric
- [ ] Skipped stitches
- [ ] Layers feed unevenly
- [x] It creases easily
- [x] Won't hold a crease

Cost per yard
- [ ] Less than $10
- [ ] $10 to $20
- [x] $20 to $30
- [ ] $30 to $40
- [ ] $40 to $50
- [ ] More than $50

Double cloth
Double cloth is a term used to describe fabrics woven with two distinct layers that are joined by an extra set of filling or warp yarns. In some cases, the two layers are cut apart, a fast, economical way to produce pile fabrics, such as velvet and corduroy. On other versions, like matelassé, the layers work together to create a special effect, and can't be separated without damaging the fabric. Some double cloths are reversible; the two sides may be made with different weaves, yarns, colors and/or patterns. Double cloth is usually a substantial, heavy fabric, but the weight varies.

Wearability
- [ ] Durable [ ] Fragile
- [x] Strong [ ] Weak
- [ ] It is long-wearing
- [ ] It wears evenly
- [ ] It wears out along seams and folds
- [ ] Seams don't hold up under stress
- [x] Fabric is subject to abrasion
- [ ] It resists abrasion
- [x] Subject to snags
- [ ] It resists snags
- [ ] Subject to runs
- [ ] It tends to pill
- [ ] It tends to shed
- [ ] It attracts lint
- [ ] It attracts static
- [ ] It is static-free
- [ ] It tends to cling
- [x] It holds its shape
- [ ] It loses its shape
- [ ] It stretches out of shape easily
- [ ] It droops, bags
- [ ] It tends to wrinkle
- [x] It resists wrinkles
- [ ] It crushes easily
- [ ] Water drops leave spots or marks

Suggested care
- [ ] Dryclean only
- [ ] Do not dryclean
- [x] Dryclean or wash
- [ ] Gently handwash in lukewarm water
- [ ] Roll in a towel to remove moisture
- [ ] Drip dry
- [ ] Lay flat to dry
- [x] Machine wash
  - [x] gentle/delicate
  - [ ] regular/normal
  - [ ] do not spin
- [x] Machine dry
  - [x] cool [ ] normal
  - [ ] perm. press
- [ ] Press damp fabric
- [ ] Press dry fabric
- [ ] Dry iron [ ] Steam
- [ ] Iron on wrong side
- [ ] Use a press cloth
- [ ] Use a needleboard
- [x] Needs no ironing
- [ ] Do not iron
- [x] Fabric may shrink
- [x] May bleed or fade

Where to find
- [ ] Any fabric store
- [ ] Major chain store
- [x] Stores that carry high quality fabric
- [x] Fabric club
- [x] Mail order
- [x] Wholesale supplier

ATTACH SAMPLE HERE

LENGTHWISE GRAIN

Matka has a coarse, homespun look.

matka

Coarsely woven fabric made in India of spun silk, usually on small, hand-operated looms. Matka is made with thick, irregular yarns in a loose plain weave or basket weave. It is heavier than most silk fabrics and has an uneven, homespun appearance, often with a dulled luster. It varies in weight, but is usually a medium to heavy fabric. Some versions are woven with multi-colored yarns, but matka is usually solid in color. Good quality matka will be evenly woven, while a lesser quality fabric may have thick or thin spots and show signs of abrasion.

How to use

Matka does not pleat, tuck or gather well. It falls away from the body and will hold the shape of the garment. Choose styles that eliminate bulk, such as tailored, fitted or semi-fitted suits, jackets and skirts. Fabric resists wrinkles and travels well, but spun yarns are subject to abrasion and looser weaves tend to snag and unravel. Drycleaning is recommended, especially if the garment has lots of inner construction.

Linen lookalikes

Matka is sometimes called silk linen, a contradictory label that confuses most consumers. In fact, the word "linen" is used to describe a number of fabrics that look like linen, but are not. Real linen is quite lustrous and luxurious. It is spun from flax, a plant fiber cultivated in Belgium, Ireland and elsewhere. This highly absorbent fiber dries quickly, making it cool and comfortable in summer, but it will never win a popularity contest because it wrinkles easily. Most imitation linen is made of rayon.

silk cashmere

A soft, thick, finely twilled fabric given a soft finish on one side only, to imitate the softness of cashmere. The fabric may be all silk or have a silk warp and a wool filling. Also called cashmere silk and cachemire de soie. Rayon cashmere is the same thing, made with rayon instead of silk.

silk cotton

A type of fiber that is neither cotton nor silk, obtained from the seed pods of various plants and trees. The silky fiber is smooth, straight and short, while true cotton fibers are thicker, corded and twisted. Silk cotton is difficult to spin, so it is used most often for stuffing.

silk linen

A confusing label used to describe all-silk fabrics that look like linen, such as matka, as well as a variety fabrics made from a blend of spun silk and linen. In general, silk/linen blends are stiffer than all-silk fabrics and tend to wrinkle more, while all-silk fabrics are more lustrous, but less durable.

Sewing rating
- ☐ Easy to sew
- ☒ Moderately easy
- ☐ Average
- ☐ Moderately difficult
- ☐ Extremely difficult

Suggested fit
- ☐ Stretch to fit
- ☐ Close-fitting
- ☒ Fitted
- ☒ Semi-fitted
- ☐ Loose-fitting
- ☐ Very loose-fitting

Suggested styles
- ☐ Pleats ☐ Tucks
  - ☐ pressed
  - ☐ unpressed
- ☐ Gathers
  - ☐ limp ☐ soft
  - ☐ full ☐ lofty
  - ☐ bouffant
- ☐ Elasticized shirring
- ☐ Smocked
- ☒ Tailored
- ☒ Shaped with seams to eliminate bulk
- ☒ Lined
- ☐ Unlined
- ☐ Puffed or bouffant
- ☐ Loose and full
- ☐ Soft and flowing
- ☐ Draped
- ☐ Cut on bias
- ☐ Stretch styling

What to expect
- ☐ Fabric is slippery, difficult to control
- ☒ It is easy to cut out
- ☐ Difficult to cut out
- ☐ Fabric has a nap
- ☒ Fabric is reversible
- ☒ Both sides of fabric look the same
- ☐ It stretches easily
- ☐ It will not stretch
- ☐ It is difficult to ease sleeves and curves
- ☐ Fabric tears easily
- ☐ It is difficult to tear
- ☒ Fabric will not tear
- ☐ Pins and needles leave holes, marks
- ☐ It tends to pucker
- ☐ It tends to unravel
- ☐ Fabric won't unravel
- ☐ Inner construction shows from outside
- ☐ Machine eats fabric
- ☐ Skipped stitches
- ☐ Layers feed unevenly
- ☐ It creases easily
- ☒ Won't hold a crease

Cost per yard
- ☐ Less than $10
- ☒ $10 to $20
- ☒ $20 to $30
- ☐ $30 to $40
- ☐ $40 to $50
- ☐ More than $50

The basket weave
Linen-look fabrics are often made with the basket weave, a variation of the plain weave produced by grouping yarns and weaving them as one. The simplest version is the 2x2 basket weave, made by pairing yarns in both directions, but there are many variations. A semi-basket weave, such as cotton oxford cloth, has yarns grouped in only one direction (2x1). A plain basket weave has square blocks; a fancy basket weave has oblong blocks. Fabrics tend to be loosely woven and resist wrinkles. Monk's cloth and homespun are examples of basket weaves.

Wearability
- ☐ Durable ☐ Fragile
- ☐ Strong ☐ Weak
- ☐ It is long-wearing
- ☒ It wears evenly
- ☐ It wears out along seams and folds
- ☐ Seams don't hold up under stress
- ☒ Fabric is subject to abrasion
- ☐ It resists abrasion
- ☒ Subject to snags
- ☐ It resists snags
- ☐ Subject to runs
- ☒ It tends to pill
- ☐ It tends to shed
- ☐ It attracts lint
- ☐ It attracts static
- ☐ It is static-free
- ☐ It tends to cling
- ☐ It holds its shape
- ☐ It loses its shape
- ☐ It stretches out of shape easily
- ☐ It droops, bags
- ☐ It tends to wrinkle
- ☒ It resists wrinkles
- ☐ It crushes easily
- ☐ Water drops leave spots or marks

Suggested care
- ☒ Dryclean only
- ☐ Do not dryclean
- ☐ Dryclean or wash
- ☐ Gently handwash in lukewarm water
- ☐ Roll in a towel to remove moisture
- ☐ Drip dry
- ☐ Lay flat to dry
- ☐ Machine wash
  - ☐ gentle/delicate
  - ☐ regular/normal
  - ☐ do not spin
- ☐ Machine dry
  - ☐ cool ☐ normal
  - ☐ perm. press
- ☐ Press damp fabric
- ☒ Press dry fabric
- ☐ Dry iron ☒ Steam
- ☐ Iron on wrong side
- ☒ Use a press cloth
- ☐ Use a needleboard
- ☐ Needs no ironing
- ☐ Do not iron
- ☒ Fabric may shrink
- ☐ May bleed or fade

Where to find
- ☐ Any fabric store
- ☐ Major chain store
- ☒ Stores that carry high quality fabric
- ☐ Fabric club
- ☒ Mail order
- ☒ Wholesale supplier

ATTACH SAMPLE HERE

LENGTHWISE GRAIN

Noil typically has dark random flecks.

noil

A dull, slightly nubby fabric with random dark or light flecks and slight crosswise ribs. It is made from silk noils, very short waste fibers from the inner part of the cocoon that are spun into yarn, usually with bits of the cocoon in it. Fabric looks more like cotton than silk. A typical noil is made with a balanced, plain weave and looks the same on both sides. It is often called raw silk, but this is inaccurate – the silk waste must be at least partially degummed before it can be spun into yarn.

How to use

Silk noil has a moderately gentle drape that maintains a soft silhouette of the garment. It may be lightly tucked, pleated or gathered, but too much fabric creates bulk. Noil resists wrinkles and travels well, but is not as strong as other silks and does not wear as well. Use to make fitted, semi-fitted or loose-fitting styles of skirts, shorts, slacks, dresses, lightweight suits and casual jackets. Dryclean or handwash and line dry, but beware of shrinkage, especially in the lengthwise direction.

Raw silk

Silk noil is frequently called raw silk, but the label is inaccurate. Raw silk is any silk that has not been cleaned of its sericin, a natural gum that holds the cocoon together and protects the fiber. Silk is rarely used in this form. The gum is usually removed by boiling the silk yarn or fabric in a soapy solution. Raw silk is quite stiff and dull. When the gum is removed, silk is softer and more lustrous. Raw silk is less desirable – the gum attracts dirt and odors and may cause an allergic reaction.

---

noil faille
Noil with very distinct crosswise ribs, made with fine warp yarns and heavy filling yarns. Fabric is much heavier than a true faille.

noil jacquard
A typically dull noil fabric with a lustrous jacquard pattern, made with satin floats.

bourette silk
A coarse, lumpy, irregular yarn spun from waste produced in the manufacture of schappe silk and from waste not suitable for spinning into schappe yarn. Often has random tufts from the nubs, noil and other waste, producing a fancy, novel effect with bright spots of color.

carded silk
Waste silk, usually from imperfect cocoons, that is carded and spun into yarn.

schappe silk
Yarn spun from silk waste that has been only partially degummed, by schapping, or fermenting, rather than boiling the silk.

Sewing rating
- ☒ Easy to sew
- ☐ Moderately easy
- ☐ Average
- ☐ Moderately difficult
- ☐ Extremely difficult

Suggested fit
- ☐ Stretch to fit
- ☐ Close-fitting
- ☒ Fitted
- ☒ Semi-fitted
- ☒ Loose-fitting
- ☐ Very loose-fitting

Suggested styles
- ☒ Pleats ☒ Tucks
  - ☐ pressed
  - ☒ unpressed
- ☒ Gathers
  - ☐ limp ☐ soft
  - ☒ full ☐ lofty
  - ☐ bouffant
- ☐ Elasticized shirring
- ☐ Smocked
- ☒ Tailored
- ☒ Shaped with seams to eliminate bulk
- ☒ Lined
- ☒ Unlined
- ☐ Puffed or bouffant
- ☒ Loose and full
- ☐ Soft and flowing
- ☐ Draped
- ☐ Cut on bias
- ☐ Stretch styling

What to expect
- ☐ Fabric is slippery, difficult to control
- ☒ It is easy to cut out
- ☐ Difficult to cut out
- ☐ Fabric has a nap
- ☒ Fabric is reversible
- ☒ Both sides of fabric look the same
- ☐ It stretches easily
- ☐ It will not stretch
- ☐ It is difficult to ease sleeves and curves
- ☐ Fabric tears easily
- ☒ It is difficult to tear
- ☐ Fabric will not tear
- ☐ Pins and needles leave holes, marks
- ☐ It tends to pucker
- ☒ It tends to unravel
- ☐ Fabric won't unravel
- ☐ Inner construction shows from outside
- ☐ Machine eats fabric
- ☐ Skipped stitches
- ☐ Layers feed unevenly
- ☐ It creases easily
- ☐ Won't hold a crease

Cost per yard
- ☒ Less than $10
- ☒ $10 to $20
- ☐ $20 to $30
- ☐ $30 to $40
- ☐ $40 to $50
- ☐ More than $50

How to preshrink silk
Silk noil and many other silks should be preshrunk before you begin to cut and sew. The finished garment can then be laundered at home, a good way to avoid drycleaning bills. It's easy: Draw a tub (or sink) full of lukewarm water and mild soap. Put the fabric in the water, swish it around, then let it sit for a couple of minutes. Rinse fabric in cold water until all soap residue is gone. Roll wet fabric in a towel to remove excess moisture. Using a dry iron and a low-to-medium setting, press the fabric dry. Silk noil can also be washed and dried by machine, but it shrinks more in the dryer.

Wearability
- ☐ Durable ☐ Fragile
- ☐ Strong ☒ Weak
- ☐ It is long-wearing
- ☒ It wears evenly
- ☐ It wears out along seams and folds
- ☐ Seams don't hold up under stress
- ☒ Fabric is subject to abrasion
- ☐ It resists abrasion
- ☐ Subject to snags
- ☐ It resists snags
- ☐ Subject to runs
- ☒ It tends to pill
- ☐ It tends to shed
- ☐ It attracts lint
- ☐ It attracts static
- ☐ It is static-free
- ☐ It tends to cling
- ☒ It holds its shape
- ☐ It loses its shape
- ☐ It stretches out of shape easily
- ☐ It droops, bags
- ☐ It tends to wrinkle
- ☒ It resists wrinkles
- ☐ It crushes easily
- ☐ Water drops leave spots or marks

Suggested care
- ☐ Dryclean only
- ☐ Do not dryclean
- ☒ Dryclean or wash
- ☒ Gently handwash in lukewarm water
- ☒ Roll in a towel to remove moisture
- ☒ Drip dry
- ☐ Lay flat to dry
- ☒ Machine wash
  - ☒ gentle/delicate
  - ☐ regular/normal
  - ☐ do not spin
- ☒ Machine dry
  - ☒ cool ☐ normal
  - ☐ perm. press
- ☒ Press damp fabric
- ☐ Press dry fabric
- ☒ Dry iron ☐ Steam
- ☐ Iron on wrong side
- ☐ Use a press cloth
- ☐ Use a needleboard
- ☐ Needs no ironing
- ☐ Do not iron
- ☒ Fabric may shrink
- ☒ May bleed or fade

Where to find
- ☐ Any fabric store
- ☒ Major chain store
- ☒ Stores that carry high quality fabric
- ☒ Fabric club
- ☒ Mail order
- ☒ Wholesale supplier

LENGTHWISE GRAIN

Silk organza is crisp and very sheer.

organza

A very sheer, crisp fabric made with a loose plain weave and tightly twisted yarns that have 10 to 20 turns per inch. It is fine to lightweight (6mm to 8mm), strong, stable and durable, with a firm, delicate hand and a flat, smooth texture. Fabric may crush or muss, but crispness is easily restored with an iron. Organza is usually not very expensive, but it is often used as a background for embroidered, flocked or tufted fabrics, which can be costly.

How to use

Organza has a crisp drape that falls away from the body in wide cones. It may be gathered or shirred into a puffed or bouffant fullness. Special sewing techniques are required for seams, facings and hems because they can be seen from the outside of the garment. Use alone or under or over a second fabric to make fitted, semi-fitted or loose-fitting styles of blouses, dresses, children's dresses and evening wear. Use to make facings, interfacings and/or linings for lightweight or sheer fabrics. Use as an underlining to add crispness and/or weight to limp, thin fabrics or to stabilize loose weaves.

Organdy

Organza is often confused with organdy, but the fabrics are different. Organza is made of silk, while organdy is cotton. Authentic organdy is a very light, thin, stiff and wiry cotton fabric treated with a chemical finish to maintain the fabric's crispness through repeated launderings. The distinction is blurred because organdy is sometimes made of silk and treated with a similar chemical finish. Silk organdy is stiffer than organza and more opaque, but has similar uses.

---

gauze

A sheer, thin, open-weave fabric made with a plain, leno or gauze weave. Silk gauze is sometimes called organza and vice versa, but authentic gauze is not as crisp and is more loosely woven. The more common cotton version is used to make lightweight summer clothing and surgical dressings.

gazar

Sheer, crisp silk fabric that is shiny on one side and dull on the other. Gazar looks like heavy organza, but it is more tightly woven and more stable. The expensive fabric may be plain, printed or woven with jacquard figures. It is sometimes used by tailors as interfacing in lightweight summer suits.

voile

A lightweight, sheer fabric with a crisp, wiry hand, made of hard-twist yarns in a loose, plain weave that usually has the same number of yarns in both directions. May be silk, cotton, wool, rayon or acetate. Fabrics may be solid in color, printed, flocked or woven with colored, lengthwise stripes.

Sewing rating
- ☐ Easy to sew
- ☒ Moderately easy
- ☐ Average
- ☐ Moderately difficult
- ☐ Extremely difficult

Suggested fit
- ☐ Stretch to fit
- ☐ Close-fitting
- ☒ Fitted
- ☒ Semi-fitted
- ☒ Loose-fitting
- ☐ Very loose-fitting

Suggested styles
- ☒ Pleats ☒ Tucks
  - ☒ pressed
  - ☐ unpressed
- ☒ Gathers
  - ☐ limp ☐ soft
  - ☐ full ☒ lofty
  - ☐ bouffant
- ☒ Elasticized shirring
- ☐ Smocked
- ☐ Tailored
- ☐ Shaped with seams to eliminate bulk
- ☒ Lined
- ☐ Unlined
- ☒ Puffed or bouffant
- ☐ Loose and full
- ☐ Soft and flowing
- ☐ Draped
- ☐ Cut on bias
- ☐ Stretch styling

What to expect
- ☐ Fabric is slippery, difficult to control
- ☐ It is easy to cut out
- ☐ Difficult to cut out
- ☐ Fabric has a nap
- ☒ Fabric is reversible
- ☒ Both sides of fabric look the same
- ☐ It stretches easily
- ☐ It will not stretch
- ☐ It is difficult to ease sleeves and curves
- ☒ Fabric tears easily
- ☐ It is difficult to tear
- ☐ Fabric will not tear
- ☐ Pins and needles leave holes, marks
- ☐ It tends to pucker
- ☐ It tends to unravel
- ☐ Fabric won't unravel
- ☒ Inner construction shows from outside
- ☐ Machine eats fabric
- ☐ Skipped stitches
- ☐ Layers feed unevenly
- ☒ It creases easily
- ☐ Won't hold a crease

Cost per yard
- ☒ Less than $10
- ☒ $10 to $20
- ☐ $20 to $30
- ☐ $30 to $40
- ☐ $40 to $50
- ☐ More than $50

Figure weaves
Organza is often used as a background for tufted, embroidered or embellished fabrics. Most of the special effects are made with various figure weaves, including the lappet, the swivel and the clip spot/dot weave. Each uses a special loom attachment to weave extra yarns into the fabric at regular intervals. These costly embellishments are widely imitated with flocking, which uses adhesive to apply raised, fuzzy dots or patterns to fabrics. More complex embellishments such as cutwork and embroidery are produced on the more well-known jacquard loom.

Wearability
- ☒ Durable ☐ Fragile
- ☒ Strong ☐ Weak
- ☐ It is long-wearing
- ☒ It wears evenly
- ☐ It wears out along seams and folds
- ☐ Seams don't hold up under stress
- ☐ Fabric is subject to abrasion
- ☐ It resists abrasion
- ☐ Subject to snags
- ☒ It resists snags
- ☐ Subject to runs
- ☐ It tends to pill
- ☐ It tends to shed
- ☐ It attracts lint
- ☐ It attracts static
- ☐ It is static-free
- ☐ It tends to cling
- ☒ It holds its shape
- ☐ It loses its shape
- ☐ It stretches out of shape easily
- ☐ It droops, bags
- ☒ It tends to wrinkle
- ☐ It resists wrinkles
- ☒ It crushes easily
- ☒ Water drops leave spots or marks

Suggested care
- ☐ Dryclean only
- ☐ Do not dryclean
- ☒ Dryclean or wash
- ☒ Gently handwash in lukewarm water
- ☒ Roll in a towel to remove moisture
- ☐ Drip dry
- ☐ Lay flat to dry
- ☐ Machine wash
  - ☐ gentle/delicate
  - ☐ regular/normal
  - ☐ do not spin
- ☐ Machine dry
  - ☐ cool ☐ normal
  - ☐ perm. press
- ☒ Press damp fabric
- ☐ Press dry fabric
- ☒ Dry iron ☐ Steam
- ☐ Iron on wrong side
- ☐ Use a press cloth
- ☐ Use a needleboard
- ☐ Needs no ironing
- ☐ Do not iron
- ☒ Fabric may shrink
- ☒ May bleed or fade

Where to find
- ☐ Any fabric store
- ☒ Major chain store
- ☒ Stores that carry high quality fabric
- ☐ Fabric club
- ☒ Mail order
- ☒ Wholesale supplier

ATTACH SAMPLE HERE

LENGTHWISE GRAIN

Peau de soie has a dull, satiny sheen.

peau de soie

French for "skin of silk." A medium-weight, smooth, silky fabric with a semi-dull finish, originally made in Padua, Italy, where it was called paduasoy, a contraction of Padua silk. Today's peau de soie looks like satin, but is actually made with a compact plain weave. It has very fine crosswise ribs, a semi-crisp hand and a satiny sheen. This firm, strong fabric is very expensive and difficult to find. A less expensive version of peau de soie has a lustrous face and a dull back, made with the satin weave. Both versions often need to be ordered in advance.

How to use

Peau de soie has a moderately stiff drape that falls into wide cones. Fabric holds the shape of the garment, and may be gathered into a lofty fullness, but the compact weave is difficult to ease. The more common satin version is subject to scuffs and abrasions. Choose close-fitting, fitted or semi-fitted styles to make bridal gowns, evening clothes and special occasion dresses. Should be drycleaned to avoid scuffs and abrasions.

Silk veiling

The best way to top off a silk bridal gown is with a soft, sheer veil made of silk tulle or illusion. The finest, most transparent veiling is called illusion; the term applies to very fine versions of all types of net fabrics. Tulle is the finest net, a delicate mesh with a small, hexagonal-shaped hole. It may be cotton or nylon, but silk is the most beautiful. It looks fragile, but is surprisingly strong. Silk tulle/illusion may be purchased from businesses that specialize in silk and other fine fabrics. It is very expensive.

---

double-face satin
Reversible fabric with a smooth satin face on both sides.

duchess satin
A very heavy, stiff, highly lustrous satin with a plain back, usually made of silk, rayon, acetate or a silk/rayon blend.

peau d' ange
French for "skin of an angel." A medium- to heavyweight satin with a dull finish, usually made of silk. It is heavier than peau de soie.

peau de cynge
French for "swan skin." A lustrous, pebbled, heavy silk satin, made with crepe yarns.

poult-de-soie
A tightly woven, stiff silk fabric with fine crosswise ribs and the rustle of taffeta.

royal satin
A fine quality, double-faced silk dress fabric, made with a twill weave and given a lustrous finish. Also called satin royale.

Sewing rating
- [ ] Easy to sew
- [ ] Moderately easy
- [x] Average
- [ ] Moderately difficult
- [ ] Extremely difficult

Suggested fit
- [ ] Stretch to fit
- [x] Close-fitting
- [x] Fitted
- [x] Semi-fitted
- [ ] Loose-fitting
- [ ] Very loose-fitting

Suggested styles
- [ ] Pleats [ ] Tucks
  - [ ] pressed
  - [ ] unpressed
- [x] Gathers
  - [ ] limp [ ] soft
  - [ ] full [x] lofty
  - [x] bouffant
- [ ] Elasticized shirring
- [ ] Smocked
- [ ] Tailored
- [x] Shaped with seams to eliminate bulk
- [x] Lined
- [x] Unlined
- [x] Puffed or bouffant
- [ ] Loose and full
- [ ] Soft and flowing
- [ ] Draped
- [ ] Cut on bias
- [ ] Stretch styling

What to expect
- [ ] Fabric is slippery, difficult to control
- [x] It is easy to cut out
- [ ] Difficult to cut out
- [ ] Fabric has a nap
- [ ] Fabric is reversible
- [ ] Both sides of fabric look the same
- [ ] It stretches easily
- [x] It will not stretch
- [x] It is difficult to ease sleeves and curves
- [ ] Fabric tears easily
- [ ] It is difficult to tear
- [x] Fabric will not tear
- [x] Pins and needles leave holes, marks
- [ ] It tends to pucker
- [ ] It tends to unravel
- [ ] Fabric won't unravel
- [ ] Inner construction shows from outside
- [ ] Machine eats fabric
- [ ] Skipped stitches
- [ ] Layers feed unevenly
- [ ] It creases easily
- [ ] Won't hold a crease

Cost per yard
- [ ] Less than $10
- [ ] $10 to $20
- [x] $20 to $30
- [x] $30 to $40
- [x] $40 to $50
- [ ] More than $50

Net fabrics
Silk tulle and other net fabrics are made by knotting, twisting or fusing intersecting yarns together. The airy, open-mesh fabric was originally made with hand-tied knots at each point of intersection. Today, net fabrics are made on special machines that can reproduce or imitate the hand-knotted net. The shape and size of the mesh varies. Net is categorized and named by degree of fineness, measured in points per inch. The greater the point count, the finer the hole. Net is often used as a background for lace, embroidery or beading. It is strong and durable.

Wearability
- [x] Durable [ ] Fragile
- [x] Strong [ ] Weak
- [ ] It is long-wearing
- [ ] It wears evenly
- [ ] It wears out along seams and folds
- [ ] Seams don't hold up under stress
- [x] Fabric is subject to abrasion
- [ ] It resists abrasion
- [x] Subject to snags
- [ ] It resists snags
- [ ] Subject to runs
- [ ] It tends to pill
- [ ] It tends to shed
- [ ] It attracts lint
- [ ] It attracts static
- [ ] It is static-free
- [ ] It tends to cling
- [x] It holds its shape
- [ ] It loses its shape
- [ ] It stretches out of shape easily
- [ ] It droops, bags
- [ ] It tends to wrinkle
- [x] It resists wrinkles
- [ ] It crushes easily
- [x] Water drops leave spots or marks

Suggested care
- [x] Dryclean only
- [ ] Do not dryclean
- [ ] Dryclean or wash
- [ ] Gently handwash in lukewarm water
- [ ] Roll in a towel to remove moisture
- [ ] Drip dry
- [ ] Lay flat to dry
- [ ] Machine wash
  - [ ] gentle/delicate
  - [ ] regular/normal
  - [ ] do not spin
- [ ] Machine dry
  - [ ] cool [ ] normal
  - [ ] perm. press
- [ ] Press damp fabric
- [x] Press dry fabric
- [x] Dry iron [ ] Steam
- [x] Iron on wrong side
- [x] Use a press cloth
- [ ] Use a needleboard
- [ ] Needs no ironing
- [ ] Do not iron
- [ ] Fabric may shrink
- [ ] May bleed or fade

Where to find
- [ ] Any fabric store
- [ ] Major chain store
- [x] Stores that carry high quality fabric
- [ ] Fabric club
- [x] Mail order
- [x] Wholesale supplier

pongee

From the Chinese word "penchi," meaning "woven at home" or "home loom." A natural, tan or cream-colored fabric with a lightly textured surface, made with a tight, plain weave from reeled tussah or other wild silk. Fabric has a dull sheen and a firm, soft or slightly crisp hand. It usually has slight random slubs in both directions, unless cultivated silk is used for the warp. The fabric's weight ranges from 5mm to 12mm, but pongee is usually lighter in weight than its cousin, shantung. Names such as Honan, Nanshan and Vonshan indicate the area in China where the fabric is made.

How to use

Pongee has a soft drape that falls into moderately soft flares. It may be shirred, gathered or pleated into a soft fullness. Pongee is durable, stable and resists snagging, but it may shrink and/or unravel. Choose semi-fitted, loose-fitting or very loose-fitting styles to make blouses and lightweight dresses. Dryclean or gently wash by hand, but beware of shrinkage.

ATTACH SAMPLE HERE

LENGTHWISE GRAIN

Pongee is usually natural in color.

Honan silk

Honan silk is a type of pongee of excellent quality from the Honan region of China, known for dyeing well, in contrast to other pongee fabrics. Honan is the only wild silk that dyes uniformly, so fabrics are often brilliantly colored or iridescent. Like other pongees, Honan is a lightweight fabric with random, slightly slubbed yarns in both directions. Honan is durable, stable and resists snagging, but the fabric may shrink and bright colors may bleed or fade. Drycleaning is recommended.

Bengal pongee
A fine silk pongee made in India.

crepe Algerian
Printed pongee with a rough, crepe texture.

crepe Berber
A textured, crepe-like pongee that is dyed.

Fuji pongee
Made from spun yarns of tussah silk.

imperial pongee
A rich, lustrous, pongee dress fabric.

Japanese pongee
A British term for habutai.

Nanshan pongee
Trade name for a pongee made from silk cultivated in the neighborhood of Chefoo. Once woven locally, now made elsewhere.

Swiss pongee
Term used in Great Britain for mercerized cotton fabric that resembles silk habutai.

Sewing rating
- [ ] Easy to sew
- [x] Moderately easy
- [ ] Average
- [ ] Moderately difficult
- [ ] Extremely difficult

Suggested fit
- [ ] Stretch to fit
- [ ] Close-fitting
- [ ] Fitted
- [x] Semi-fitted
- [x] Loose-fitting
- [x] Very loose-fitting

Suggested styles
- [x] Pleats [x] Tucks
  - [x] pressed
  - [ ] unpressed
- [x] Gathers
  - [ ] limp [x] soft
  - [ ] full [ ] lofty
  - [ ] bouffant
- [x] Elasticized shirring
- [ ] Smocked
- [ ] Tailored
- [ ] Shaped with seams to eliminate bulk
- [ ] Lined
- [ ] Unlined
- [ ] Puffed or bouffant
- [x] Loose and full
- [x] Soft and flowing
- [ ] Draped
- [ ] Cut on bias
- [ ] Stretch styling

What to expect
- [ ] Fabric is slippery, difficult to control
- [x] It is easy to cut out
- [ ] Difficult to cut out
- [ ] Fabric has a nap
- [x] Fabric is reversible
- [x] Both sides of fabric look the same
- [ ] It stretches easily
- [ ] It will not stretch
- [x] It is difficult to ease sleeves and curves
- [x] Fabric tears easily
- [ ] It is difficult to tear
- [ ] Fabric will not tear
- [ ] Pins and needles leave holes, marks
- [ ] It tends to pucker
- [x] It tends to unravel
- [ ] Fabric won't unravel
- [ ] Inner construction shows from outside
- [ ] Machine eats fabric
- [ ] Skipped stitches
- [ ] Layers feed unevenly
- [ ] It creases easily
- [ ] Won't hold a crease

Cost per yard
- [x] Less than $10
- [x] $10 to $20
- [ ] $20 to $30
- [ ] $30 to $40
- [ ] $40 to $50
- [ ] More than $50

Fading and bleeding
Honan and other silk fabrics are often dyed brilliant colors, but the colors tend to fade or bleed if the fabric gets wet. Technically, this is merely the loss of excess dye, but the results may be disastrous, especially if several colors run together. To test for colorfastness, place a few drops of warm, soapy water on the fabric or garment in an inconspicuous place. Wait a bit, then blot with a clean, white cloth. If the silk or the cloth turns color, it would be wise to have the fabric drycleaned. To handwash fabrics that bleed, add 1/4 cup of white vinegar or salt to lukewarm, soapy water for every wash, then wash and dry quickly.

Wearability
- [x] Durable [ ] Fragile
- [x] Strong [ ] Weak
- [x] It is long-wearing
- [x] It wears evenly
- [ ] It wears out along seams and folds
- [ ] Seams don't hold up under stress
- [ ] Fabric is subject to abrasion
- [ ] It resists abrasion
- [ ] Subject to snags
- [x] It resists snags
- [ ] Subject to runs
- [ ] It tends to pill
- [ ] It tends to shed
- [ ] It attracts lint
- [ ] It attracts static
- [ ] It is static-free
- [ ] It tends to cling
- [x] It holds its shape
- [ ] It loses its shape
- [ ] It stretches out of shape easily
- [ ] It droops, bags
- [ ] It tends to wrinkle
- [ ] It resists wrinkles
- [ ] It crushes easily
- [ ] Water drops leave spots or marks

Suggested care
- [ ] Dryclean only
- [ ] Do not dryclean
- [x] Dryclean or wash
- [x] Gently handwash in lukewarm water
- [x] Roll in a towel to remove moisture
- [x] Drip dry
- [ ] Lay flat to dry
- [ ] Machine wash
  - [ ] gentle/delicate
  - [ ] regular/normal
  - [ ] do not spin
- [ ] Machine dry
  - [ ] cool [ ] normal
  - [ ] perm. press
- [x] Press damp fabric
- [ ] Press dry fabric
- [x] Dry iron [ ] Steam
- [ ] Iron on wrong side
- [ ] Use a press cloth
- [ ] Use a needleboard
- [ ] Needs no ironing
- [ ] Do not iron
- [x] Fabric may shrink
- [x] May bleed or fade

Where to find
- [ ] Any fabric store
- [ ] Major chain store
- [x] Stores that carry high quality fabric
- [ ] Fabric club
- [x] Mail order
- [x] Wholesale supplier

ATTACH SAMPLE HERE

LENGTHWISE GRAIN

This printed jacquard is not reversible.

printed silk

Any silk fabric that has been printed with a colored design or pattern. Cultivated silk prints beautifully – the back side often looks as good as the front. The best results are achieved when the design is printed on a plain, smooth fabric, such as crepe de Chine or charmeuse. Other printed silks include chiffon, faille, georgette, jacquard, surah and sometimes, taffeta. The price varies considerably, depending on the type of fabric, quality and country of origin. Italian and Japanese prints are the most beautiful, and usually, the most expensive.

Screen prints

Screen printing is an expensive, labor-intensive form of printing. The unprinted fabric is unrolled on a long, flat surface. A design is etched out on a nylon screen, which is stretched taut over a small wooden frame. The frame is placed over the fabric and a squeegee is used to squeeze colored goo through the screen onto the fabric. A new screen is used for each color. The dye must be dry before the next color is applied. The process is called silk screening because the screens were once made of silk.

How to use

Printed silk often has a beautiful drape and usually may be gathered, shirred or pleated into a soft fullness, depending on the type of fabric. Some prints have a one-way design that requires a "with nap" cutting layout; other prints may be unsuitable for use on the bias. Choose semi-fitted, loose or very loose styles to make blouses, skirts, slacks, dresses and scarves. Drycleaning is recommended to preserve the intensity of the colors and to avoid bleeding.

Como silk
A general term for luxurious fabrics from Como, the silk center of Italy. Italian mills import raw silk filament from Japan and China, but weave and print their own fabrics. Some mills even print silks for Japanese firms. The term is often used to describe prints used to make expensive men's ties.

printed jacquard
Interesting combinations are created when a second design is printed over jacquard's dull-and-lustrous woven pattern. On some versions, the woven pattern adds subtle spots of luster to a dominant or colorful print. On others, the print adds spots of color to an elaborate woven pattern.

sandwashed prints
Any printed silk that has been treated to an abrasive wash, creating a soft, velvety fabric with a supple bounce and a subdued luster. Colors are usually muted and print may be slightly blurred, rather than sharp and clear. Unlike other silk prints, this fabric can be laundered at home.

Sewing rating
- ☐ Easy to sew
- ☐ Moderately easy
- ☒ Average
- ☐ Moderately difficult
- ☐ Extremely difficult

Suggested fit
- ☐ Stretch to fit
- ☐ Close-fitting
- ☐ Fitted
- ☒ Semi-fitted
- ☒ Loose-fitting
- ☒ Very loose-fitting

Suggested styles
- ☒ Pleats ☒ Tucks
  - ☒ pressed
  - ☒ unpressed
- ☒ Gathers
  - ☒ limp ☒ soft
  - ☐ full ☐ lofty
  - ☐ bouffant
- ☒ Elasticized shirring
- ☐ Smocked
- ☐ Tailored
- ☐ Shaped with seams to eliminate bulk
- ☐ Lined
- ☐ Unlined
- ☐ Puffed or bouffant
- ☒ Loose and full
- ☒ Soft and flowing
- ☒ Draped
- ☐ Cut on bias
- ☐ Stretch styling

What to expect
- ☒ Fabric is slippery, difficult to control
- ☐ It is easy to cut out
- ☐ Difficult to cut out
- ☒ Fabric has a nap
- ☐ Fabric is reversible
- ☐ Both sides of fabric look the same
- ☐ It stretches easily
- ☐ It will not stretch
- ☐ It is difficult to ease sleeves and curves
- ☐ Fabric tears easily
- ☐ It is difficult to tear
- ☐ Fabric will not tear
- ☒ Pins and needles leave holes, marks
- ☐ It tends to pucker
- ☐ It tends to unravel
- ☐ Fabric won't unravel
- ☐ Inner construction shows from outside
- ☒ Machine eats fabric
- ☐ Skipped stitches
- ☐ Layers feed unevenly
- ☐ It creases easily
- ☐ Won't hold a crease

Cost per yard
- ☐ Less than $10
- ☐ $10 to $20
- ☒ $20 to $30
- ☒ $30 to $40
- ☒ $40 to $50
- ☒ More than $50

Silk from Italy
The silk industry spread west through Italy during the 14th century and quickly became a financial base for the Renaissance. Italian weavers created exceptionally fine silk fabrics, including sumptuous brocades, intricate tapestries and luxurious cut and patterned velvets. Political troubles prompted many of the weavers to flee to France, but Italy continued to cultivate silk and produce fine woven fabrics. Italy also developed a lucrative printing industry and elevated printed silk to an art form. Today, Italy is the only significant source of raw silk remaining in Europe, but compared to China, Japan and India, its contribution is miniscule.

Wearability
- ☐ Durable ☐ Fragile
- ☐ Strong ☐ Weak
- ☐ It is long-wearing
- ☒ It wears evenly
- ☐ It wears out along seams and folds
- ☐ Seams don't hold up under stress
- ☒ Fabric is subject to abrasion
- ☐ It resists abrasion
- ☐ Subject to snags
- ☐ It resists snags
- ☐ Subject to runs
- ☐ It tends to pill
- ☐ It tends to shed
- ☐ It attracts lint
- ☒ It attracts static
- ☐ It is static-free
- ☒ It tends to cling
- ☒ It holds its shape
- ☐ It loses its shape
- ☐ It stretches out of shape easily
- ☐ It droops, bags
- ☒ It tends to wrinkle
- ☐ It resists wrinkles
- ☐ It crushes easily
- ☒ Water drops leave spots or marks

Suggested care
- ☒ Dryclean only
- ☐ Do not dryclean
- ☐ Dryclean or wash
- ☐ Gently handwash in lukewarm water
- ☐ Roll in a towel to remove moisture
- ☐ Drip dry
- ☐ Lay flat to dry
- ☐ Machine wash
  - ☐ gentle/delicate
  - ☐ regular/normal
  - ☐ do not spin
- ☐ Machine dry
  - ☐ cool ☐ normal
  - ☐ perm. press
- ☐ Press damp fabric
- ☒ Press dry fabric
- ☒ Dry iron ☐ Steam
- ☐ Iron on wrong side
- ☐ Use a press cloth
- ☐ Use a needleboard
- ☐ Needs no ironing
- ☐ Do not iron
- ☐ Fabric may shrink
- ☒ May bleed or fade

Where to find
- ☐ Any fabric store
- ☒ Major chain store
- ☒ Stores that carry high quality fabric
- ☒ Fabric club
- ☒ Mail order
- ☒ Wholesale supplier

Sandwashed charmeuse has a velvety feel.

sandwashed silk

Any silk fabric that has been treated to an abrasive wash, using sand and chemicals, in much the same way stonewashed denim is made. Fabric emerges with a soft, velvety hand, a supple bounce and a dulled luster. Sandwashed silks look and feel luxurious. Charmeuse produces the most velvety hand, but there are sandwashed versions of other silks, including broadcloth, China silk, crepe de Chine, habutai, jacquard, shantung and taffeta. Shop around — the weight, hand, appearance and quality of the fabrics vary. The price is consistently high.

How to use

Sandwashed silks have a remarkable drape and may be softly tucked, shirred or gathered, but most versions won't hold pleats. Fabric usually has a subtle, one-way luster that requires a "with nap" cutting layout. Use to make loose or very loose styles of blouses, dresses, skirts and slacks. Use heavier fabrics for lightweight suits. Fabric may be drycleaned, but the softness is enhanced when it is machine washed and dried. Press to restore smooth appearance.

Wash and beware

Not all silks are created equal — the quality of these popular fabrics varies a lot. Problems sometimes surface in the wash — fabrics may become stiff or lifeless, fade badly, or lose the soft, velvety hand, emerging as smooth, shiny reincarnations of their former selves. Changes usually can't be reversed. What to do? Shop carefully and beware of "bargains." If you're not sure, buy a small piece and run it through a series of test washes before investing money and time in a sewing project.

---

peau de suede
French for "skin of suede." A very soft silk fabric with a hand that suggests the texture of suede.

silk chamois
Trade name for a luxurious, sandwashed charmeuse that feels like very soft suede.

silk mousse
Trade name for a less costly washed silk.

silk suede
A soft leather product that feels like silk.

sueded silk
Trade name for a sandwashed charmeuse.

washed silk
Similar to sandwashed silk, but the silk is treated to a different finishing wash that produces a very soft, wrinkled fabric that can be machine washed and dried. There are many variations. The term is also used more loosely to describe any washed silk, including sandwashed silk.

Sewing rating
- [ ] Easy to sew
- [ ] Moderately easy
- [x] Average
- [ ] Moderately difficult
- [ ] Extremely difficult

Suggested fit
- [ ] Stretch to fit
- [ ] Close-fitting
- [ ] Fitted
- [x] Semi-fitted
- [x] Loose-fitting
- [x] Very loose-fitting

Suggested styles
- [ ] Pleats [x] Tucks
  - [ ] pressed
  - [x] unpressed
- [x] Gathers
  - [ ] limp [x] soft
  - [ ] full [ ] lofty
  - [ ] bouffant
- [ ] Elasticized shirring
- [ ] Smocked
- [ ] Tailored
- [ ] Shaped with seams to eliminate bulk
- [ ] Lined
- [ ] Unlined
- [ ] Puffed or bouffant
- [x] Loose and full
- [x] Soft and flowing
- [x] Draped
- [x] Cut on bias
- [ ] Stretch styling

What to expect
- [ ] Fabric is slippery, difficult to control
- [ ] It is easy to cut out
- [ ] Difficult to cut out
- [x] Fabric has a nap
- [ ] Fabric is reversible
- [ ] Both sides of fabric look the same
- [ ] It stretches easily
- [ ] It will not stretch
- [ ] It is difficult to ease sleeves and curves
- [ ] Fabric tears easily
- [x] It is difficult to tear
- [ ] Fabric will not tear
- [x] Pins and needles leave holes, marks
- [ ] It tends to pucker
- [ ] It tends to unravel
- [x] Fabric won't unravel
- [ ] Inner construction shows from outside
- [ ] Machine eats fabric
- [x] Skipped stitches
- [ ] Layers feed unevenly
- [ ] It creases easily
- [x] Won't hold a crease

Cost per yard
- [ ] Less than $10
- [ ] $10 to $20
- [x] $20 to $30
- [x] $30 to $40
- [x] $40 to $50
- [ ] More than $50

How to handwash silk

Silk tends to look dull and dingy after several trips to the cleaners. In fact, many silks actually look better and last longer when washed by hand. For best results, soak the garment in lukewarm water and a mild soap, such as Ivory Snow or a gentle shampoo. Rinse it well in cold water, then add a 1/4 cup of white vinegar to a clean rinse and rinse again. The vinegar will neutralize any soap residue and restore the silk's luster. Rinse again to remove the smell of vinegar. Roll garment in a towel to remove moisture, but do not wring. Hang to dry on a padded hanger. For best results, iron while garment is slightly damp.

VERY MILD SOAP / *WHITE VINEGAR*

Wearability
- [ ] Durable [ ] Fragile
- [ ] Strong [x] Weak
- [ ] It is long-wearing
- [ ] It wears evenly
- [x] It wears out along seams and folds
- [ ] Seams don't hold up under stress
- [x] Fabric is subject to abrasion
- [ ] It resists abrasion
- [ ] Subject to snags
- [ ] It resists snags
- [ ] Subject to runs
- [ ] It tends to pill
- [ ] It tends to shed
- [ ] It attracts lint
- [ ] It attracts static
- [ ] It is static-free
- [ ] It tends to cling
- [x] It holds its shape
- [ ] It loses its shape
- [ ] It stretches out of shape easily
- [ ] It droops, bags
- [ ] It tends to wrinkle
- [x] It resists wrinkles
- [ ] It crushes easily
- [x] Water drops leave spots or marks

Suggested care
- [ ] Dryclean only
- [ ] Do not dryclean
- [x] Dryclean or wash
- [ ] Gently handwash in lukewarm water
- [ ] Roll in a towel to remove moisture
- [ ] Drip dry
- [ ] Lay flat to dry
- [x] Machine wash
  - [x] gentle/delicate
  - [ ] regular/normal
  - [ ] do not spin
- [x] Machine dry
  - [x] cool [ ] normal
  - [ ] perm. press
- [x] Press damp fabric
- [ ] Press dry fabric
- [ ] Dry iron [ ] Steam
- [x] Iron on wrong side
- [ ] Use a press cloth
- [ ] Use a needleboard
- [ ] Needs no ironing
- [ ] Do not iron
- [ ] Fabric may shrink
- [x] May bleed or fade

Where to find
- [ ] Any fabric store
- [x] Major chain store
- [x] Stores that carry high quality fabric
- [x] Fabric club
- [x] Mail order
- [x] Wholesale supplier

61

LENGTHWISE GRAIN

Shantung silk is heavier than pongee.

shantung

A medium-light to heavy, plain-weave fabric with slight crosswise ribs and slubs. First woven in the province of Shantung, China, from hand-reeled tussah silk. Today's version is usually made with fine warp yarns of cultivated silk and heavier filling yarns of douppioni silk. Fabric has a firm, semi-crisp hand and may be lustrous or dull, depending on the quality of the yarns. Shantung is usually heavier than its cousin, pongee, but lighter in weight than douppioni, another close relative. Shot, or iridescent, versions are common.

How to use

Shantung has a semi-crisp drape that falls into moderately crisp flares. It may be gathered or pleated into a crisp fullness. Fabric is stable and resists snags, but it tends to unravel and is subject to seam slippage. Avoid close-fitting styles that put stress on seams. Choose semi-fitted, loose-fitting or very loose-fitting styles to make blouses, dresses, suits and slacks. Dryclean or gently wash by hand.

Shot silk

Shot silk is the name given to fabric woven with yarns of two different colors — one for the warp and one for the filling — producing an iridescent effect that shimmers and changes color when the fabric moves or the angle of view changes. It is usually made with very lustrous filament yarns and a balanced plain weave. The shot effect may be dramatic or subtle, depending on the colors. Honan, douppioni, taffeta and Thai silk are frequently iridescent. Also called changeable or glacé.

---

antique satin

A reversible fabric made of silk or other fibers. One side looks like shantung, with crosswise slubs; the other resembles silk satin from an earlier century.

nankeen

Another name for shantung.

rajah

A variation of shantung, originally made in India of tussah yarns.

sandwashed shantung

Shantung that has been treated to an abrasive wash, using sand and chemicals, to produce a velvety hand and dull luster.

shantung taffeta

A lightweight variation of shantung made from silk that has not been degummed. The gum, or sericin, adds weight and body to the fabric, giving it a crispness like taffeta. This fabric can accurately be called raw silk. Because raw silk is not very desirable, shantung taffeta is not very common.

Sewing rating
- [ ] Easy to sew
- [x] Moderately easy
- [ ] Average
- [ ] Moderately difficult
- [ ] Extremely difficult

Suggested fit
- [ ] Stretch to fit
- [ ] Close-fitting
- [ ] Fitted
- [x] Semi-fitted
- [x] Loose-fitting
- [x] Very loose-fitting

Suggested styles
- [x] Pleats [x] Tucks
  - [x] pressed
  - [ ] unpressed
- [x] Gathers
  - [ ] limp [x] soft
  - [x] full [ ] lofty
  - [ ] bouffant
- [ ] Elasticized shirring
- [ ] Smocked
- [ ] Tailored
- [ ] Shaped with seams to eliminate bulk
- [ ] Lined
- [ ] Unlined
- [ ] Puffed or bouffant
- [x] Loose and full
- [ ] Soft and flowing
- [ ] Draped
- [ ] Cut on bias
- [ ] Stretch styling

What to expect
- [ ] Fabric is slippery, difficult to control
- [ ] It is easy to cut out
- [ ] Difficult to cut out
- [ ] Fabric has a nap
- [x] Fabric is reversible
- [x] Both sides of fabric look the same
- [ ] It stretches easily
- [ ] It will not stretch
- [ ] It is difficult to ease sleeves and curves
- [ ] Fabric tears easily
- [x] It is difficult to tear
- [ ] Fabric will not tear
- [ ] Pins and needles leave holes, marks
- [ ] It tends to pucker
- [x] It tends to unravel
- [ ] Fabric won't unravel
- [ ] Inner construction shows from outside
- [ ] Machine eats fabric
- [ ] Skipped stitches
- [ ] Layers feed unevenly
- [ ] It creases easily
- [ ] Won't hold a crease

Cost per yard
- [ ] Less than $10
- [ ] $10 to $20
- [x] $20 to $30
- [ ] $30 to $40
- [ ] $40 to $50
- [ ] More than $50

Seam slippage
This term describes what happens when a garment pulls apart at a seam, but the seam remains intact. Slippage is actually the sliding or shifting of lengthwise yarns, prompted by tension or friction during wear or in the wash. It is sometimes caused by an improper finish or poor construction techniques, but it is more often the result of weak or flawed fabric or a poor match of fabric and style. Loose weaves, long satin floats and fabrics made with smooth yarns, like silk, are more troubled by slippage than others. Close-fitting styles increase the problem.

Wearability
- [x] Durable [ ] Fragile
- [x] Strong [ ] Weak
- [x] It is long-wearing
- [ ] It wears evenly
- [ ] It wears out along seams and folds
- [x] Seams don't hold up under stress
- [x] Fabric is subject to abrasion
- [ ] It resists abrasion
- [ ] Subject to snags
- [x] It resists snags
- [ ] Subject to runs
- [ ] It tends to pill
- [ ] It tends to shed
- [ ] It attracts lint
- [ ] It attracts static
- [ ] It is static-free
- [ ] It tends to cling
- [x] It holds its shape
- [ ] It loses its shape
- [ ] It stretches out of shape easily
- [ ] It droops, bags
- [ ] It tends to wrinkle
- [x] It resists wrinkles
- [ ] It crushes easily
- [ ] Water drops leave spots or marks

Suggested care
- [ ] Dryclean only
- [ ] Do not dryclean
- [x] Dryclean or wash
- [x] Gently handwash in lukewarm water
- [x] Roll in a towel to remove moisture
- [x] Drip dry
- [ ] Lay flat to dry
- [ ] Machine wash
  - [ ] gentle/delicate
  - [ ] regular/normal
  - [ ] do not spin
- [ ] Machine dry
  - [ ] cool [ ] normal
  - [ ] perm. press
- [x] Press damp fabric
- [ ] Press dry fabric
- [x] Dry iron [ ] Steam
- [ ] Iron on wrong side
- [ ] Use a press cloth
- [ ] Use a needleboard
- [ ] Needs no ironing
- [ ] Do not iron
- [x] Fabric may shrink
- [x] May bleed or fade

Where to find
- [ ] Any fabric store
- [x] Major chain store
- [x] Stores that carry high quality fabric
- [x] Fabric club
- [x] Mail order
- [x] Wholesale supplier

Suiting is often made of spun silk.

suiting

A group of elegant, expensive fabrics used to make suits. Fabric is often woven with novelty or slubbed yarns and/or novelty weaves to add texture and interest. Houndstooth and herringbone patterns are common. Fabric may be dull, lustrous or both, depending on the type of yarns. Suiting is usually smoother, softer and not as coarse as silk tweed, and is more tightly woven than silk linen/homespun. The silk is often blended with wool, linen, cotton, rayon or synthetic fibers.

How to use

In general, silk suitings are softer and less bulky than silk linens and tweeds. Some suitings have a moderately soft drape and can be lightly tucked or gathered, while others are moderately stiff. In most cases, the fabric holds the shape of the garment; it works best with fitted or semi-fitted styles that are shaped with seams to eliminate bulk. Novelty yarns and weaves tend to snag. Use to make tailored dresses, suits, jackets and fitted skirts. Dryclean only, especially if the garment is lined or has other inner construction.

Silk lining

A silk lining is a great way to finish the inside of a suit. Silk is strong and it breathes, so a lining made of silk won't wear out before the suit does, and it won't trap moisture against the body. Silk taffeta makes an excellent suit lining. It is durable and opaque, it won't snag, and its smooth face allows the suit to be slipped on and off with ease. China silk is too thin and fragile for suit lining. Use silk organza as an underlining to stabilize a loose weave or add weight or body to a thin fabric.

---

herringbone twill

A variation of the twill weave composed of vertical sections in which the diagonal line changes direction from left to right and back again, forming a V-shaped pattern that resembles the skeleton of a herring. The popular twill is widely used in all kinds of fabrics. Also called a chevron weave.

houndstooth check

Fabric with a pattern of pointed checks, made with a two-up, two-down broken twill weave. Widely used to make suiting fabrics.

novelty weave

Any weave that varies or combines the three basic weaves (plain, twill and satin).

novelty yarns

A general term for a wide variety of yarns with unusual or special visual effects, such as loops, beads, lumps or thick-and-thin plys. It may also refer to unusual color combinations. Novelty yarns include bouclé, curly, chenille, corkscrew, nub, seed, slub, spiral and splash, among others.

Sewing rating
- [ ] Easy to sew
- [ ] Moderately easy
- [x] Average
- [ ] Moderately difficult
- [ ] Extremely difficult

Suggested fit
- [ ] Stretch to fit
- [ ] Close-fitting
- [x] Fitted
- [x] Semi-fitted
- [ ] Loose-fitting
- [ ] Very loose-fitting

Suggested styles
- [ ] Pleats [ ] Tucks
  - [ ] pressed
  - [ ] unpressed
- [ ] Gathers
  - [ ] limp [ ] soft
  - [ ] full [ ] lofty
  - [ ] bouffant
- [ ] Elasticized shirring
- [ ] Smocked
- [x] Tailored
- [x] Shaped with seams to eliminate bulk
- [x] Lined
- [ ] Unlined
- [ ] Puffed or bouffant
- [ ] Loose and full
- [ ] Soft and flowing
- [ ] Draped
- [ ] Cut on bias
- [ ] Stretch styling

What to expect
- [ ] Fabric is slippery, difficult to control
- [x] It is easy to cut out
- [ ] Difficult to cut out
- [ ] Fabric has a nap
- [ ] Fabric is reversible
- [ ] Both sides of fabric look the same
- [ ] It stretches easily
- [ ] It will not stretch
- [x] It is difficult to ease sleeves and curves
- [ ] Fabric tears easily
- [ ] It is difficult to tear
- [x] Fabric will not tear
- [ ] Pins and needles leave holes, marks
- [ ] It tends to pucker
- [ ] It tends to unravel
- [ ] Fabric won't unravel
- [ ] Inner construction shows from outside
- [ ] Machine eats fabric
- [ ] Skipped stitches
- [ ] Layers feed unevenly
- [ ] It creases easily
- [x] Won't hold a crease

Cost per yard
- [ ] Less than $10
- [x] $10 to $20
- [x] $20 to $30
- [x] $30 to $40
- [ ] $40 to $50
- [ ] More than $50

Broken twills

Many suiting fabrics are made with a twill weave that changes direction, forming a pattern that looks like a series of points, zigzags or chevrons. The pattern, called a broken twill, may be even, like the precise, V-shaped chevrons of herringbone, or uneven, with the twill line making more random changes in direction. On some broken twills, the diagonal line is not readily apparent. On houndstooth, for example, a broken twill is used to produce a sort of ragged, checked pattern. There are many versions of broken twill, which is also called fancy, zigzag and pointed twill.

Wearability
- [ ] Durable [ ] Fragile
- [ ] Strong [ ] Weak
- [ ] It is long-wearing
- [x] It wears evenly
- [ ] It wears out along seams and folds
- [ ] Seams don't hold up under stress
- [x] Fabric is subject to abrasion
- [ ] It resists abrasion
- [ ] Subject to snags
- [ ] It resists snags
- [ ] Subject to runs
- [x] It tends to pill
- [ ] It tends to shed
- [ ] It attracts lint
- [ ] It attracts static
- [ ] It is static-free
- [ ] It tends to cling
- [x] It holds its shape
- [ ] It loses its shape
- [ ] It stretches out of shape easily
- [ ] It droops, bags
- [ ] It tends to wrinkle
- [x] It resists wrinkles
- [ ] It crushes easily
- [ ] Water drops leave spots or marks

Suggested care
- [x] Dryclean only
- [ ] Do not dryclean
- [ ] Dryclean or wash
- [ ] Gently handwash in lukewarm water
- [ ] Roll in a towel to remove moisture
- [ ] Drip dry
- [ ] Lay flat to dry
- [ ] Machine wash
  - [ ] gentle/delicate
  - [ ] regular/normal
  - [ ] do not spin
- [ ] Machine dry
  - [ ] cool [ ] normal
  - [ ] perm. press
- [ ] Press damp fabric
- [x] Press dry fabric
- [ ] Dry iron [x] Steam
- [x] Iron on wrong side
- [x] Use a press cloth
- [ ] Use a needleboard
- [ ] Needs no ironing
- [ ] Do not iron
- [ ] Fabric may shrink
- [ ] May bleed or fade

Where to find
- [ ] Any fabric store
- [ ] Major chain store
- [x] Stores that carry high quality fabric
- [x] Fabric club
- [x] Mail order
- [x] Wholesale supplier

ATTACH SAMPLE HERE

LENGTHWISE GRAIN

Surah is soft, with a diagonal twill line.

surah

A soft, lightweight silk twill fabric named for Surat, India, where it was first made. Surah is woven with slack-twist yarns, giving the fabric a semi-dull luster. It has a fine, soft, supple hand and a flat, smooth, slippery texture. A definite diagonal, or twill, line can be seen on both sides of the fabric, running from the lower left to the upper right. Surah is often printed with foulard or paisley patterns, but it may also be striped, checked, plaid or solid in color. Fabric is usually reversible unless it is printed. Also called silk twill and tie silk.

How to use

Surah has a beautiful drape that may be gathered, shirred or pleated into a soft fullness. The fabric tailors nicely, but does not wear well — it snags and scuffs easily and wears out along seams, folds and hem lines. Choose fitted, semi-fitted or loose-fitting styles to make blouses, dresses, tailored shirts, scarves and men's neckties. Surah is sometimes used for linings, but it is not very durable. Drycleaning is recommended to avoid scuffs and abrasions.

Silk foulard

Foulard is a soft, lightweight, lustrous fabric that is almost identical to surah, made with a two-up, two-down twill weave. It is generally printed with a small design on a plain background and, like surah, is used to make men's ties, handkerchiefs and women's scarves. Foulard is French for "silk handkerchief." It was originally made of silk and exported from India. Today, it is also made of worsted wool, rayon, cotton and synthetics, sometimes with a plain weave. It is also called gum twill.

Macclesfield silk

A term applied to silk fabrics made at the weaving center of Macclesfield, England, where the Huguenot weavers settled after being expelled from France. In the United States, the term is used to describe the small, neat all-over dobby patterns that are typical of tie silks from Macclesfield.

satin foulard

A smooth silk foulard with a highly lustrous finish. Foulard is not satin, but the term is meant to suggest a lustrous finish.

satin surah

A very soft surah that has been given a very lustrous finish.

Spitalfields silk

Small, neat, all-over designs, usually woven on a dobby loom. Named for Spitalfields, England, a former center for silk weaving.

tie silk

A general term for narrow silk yardage used for men's ties. Usually printed.

Sewing rating
- ☐ Easy to sew
- ☒ Moderately easy
- ☐ Average
- ☐ Moderately difficult
- ☐ Extremely difficult

Suggested fit
- ☐ Stretch to fit
- ☐ Close-fitting
- ☒ Fitted
- ☒ Semi-fitted
- ☒ Loose-fitting
- ☐ Very loose-fitting

Suggested styles
- ☒ Pleats ☒ Tucks
  - ☒ pressed
  - ☐ unpressed
- ☒ Gathers
  - ☐ limp ☒ soft
  - ☐ full ☐ lofty
  - ☐ bouffant
- ☒ Elasticized shirring
- ☐ Smocked
- ☒ Tailored
- ☐ Shaped with seams to eliminate bulk
- ☐ Lined
- ☐ Unlined
- ☐ Puffed or bouffant
- ☐ Loose and full
- ☒ Soft and flowing
- ☒ Draped
- ☒ Cut on bias
- ☐ Stretch styling

What to expect
- ☐ Fabric is slippery, difficult to control
- ☐ It is easy to cut out
- ☐ Difficult to cut out
- ☐ Fabric has a nap
- ☒ Fabric is reversible
- ☒ Both sides of fabric look the same
- ☐ It stretches easily
- ☐ It will not stretch
- ☒ It is difficult to ease sleeves and curves
- ☐ Fabric tears easily
- ☒ It is difficult to tear
- ☐ Fabric will not tear
- ☐ Pins and needles leave holes, marks
- ☐ It tends to pucker
- ☐ It tends to unravel
- ☒ Fabric won't unravel
- ☐ Inner construction shows from outside
- ☐ Machine eats fabric
- ☐ Skipped stitches
- ☐ Layers feed unevenly
- ☒ It creases easily
- ☐ Won't hold a crease

Cost per yard
- ☒ Less than $10
- ☒ $10 to $20
- ☐ $20 to $30
- ☐ $30 to $40
- ☐ $40 to $50
- ☐ More than $50

Silk from India

India's long history of silk production dates back to 200 A.D., when cultivated, white-silk producing silkworm eggs were smuggled into the country from China. India has always been home to several species of wild silk moths, and today, the country turns out large quantities of fabrics from both cultivated and wild silkworms. India produces about 20 percent of the world's silk, but it is best known for rough, tweedy, handwoven fabrics. Villagers spin and weave small amounts of silk gathered from the wild, just as they have done for centuries. Many of the fabrics are lovely, but the quality is inconsistent.

Wearability
- ☐ Durable ☐ Fragile
- ☐ Strong ☒ Weak
- ☐ It is long-wearing
- ☐ It wears evenly
- ☒ It wears out along seams and folds
- ☐ Seams don't hold up under stress
- ☒ Fabric is subject to abrasion
- ☐ It resists abrasion
- ☒ Subject to snags
- ☐ It resists snags
- ☐ Subject to runs
- ☐ It tends to pill
- ☐ It tends to shed
- ☐ It attracts lint
- ☐ It attracts static
- ☐ It is static-free
- ☐ It tends to cling
- ☐ It holds its shape
- ☐ It loses its shape
- ☐ It stretches out of shape easily
- ☐ It droops, bags
- ☒ It tends to wrinkle
- ☐ It resists wrinkles
- ☐ It crushes easily
- ☐ Water drops leave spots or marks

Suggested care
- ☒ Dryclean only
- ☐ Do not dryclean
- ☐ Dryclean or wash
- ☐ Gently handwash in lukewarm water
- ☐ Roll in a towel to remove moisture
- ☐ Drip dry
- ☐ Lay flat to dry
- ☐ Machine wash
  - ☐ gentle/delicate
  - ☐ regular/normal
  - ☐ do not spin
- ☐ Machine dry
  - ☐ cool ☐ normal
  - ☐ perm. press
- ☐ Press damp fabric
- ☒ Press dry fabric
- ☒ Dry iron ☐ Steam
- ☐ Iron on wrong side
- ☐ Use a press cloth
- ☐ Use a needleboard
- ☐ Needs no ironing
- ☐ Do not iron
- ☐ Fabric may shrink
- ☐ May bleed or fade

Where to find
- ☐ Any fabric store
- ☐ Major chain store
- ☒ Stores that carry high quality fabric
- ☐ Fabric club
- ☒ Mail order
- ☒ Wholesale supplier

```
ATTACH SAMPLE HERE
```

LENGTHWISE GRAIN

Silk taffeta is known for its rustle.

taffeta

Silk taffeta is one of the oldest luxury fabrics, woven in the early part of the third century by the Persians, who called it "taftah" or "taftan." Today's version is a fine, smooth, tightly woven fabric with very fine crosswise ribs, made with a plain weave, fine warp yarns and heavier filling yarns. Taffeta looks the same on both sides and has approximately the same number of yarns in both directions. The fabric is flat, with a distinctive rustle and a dull luster. It may be soft or stiff, and light to medium in weight. Acetate and nylon variations are common.

How to use

Silk taffeta has a crisp drape and may be gathered into a lofty fullness. Pleats hold a sharp crease. Fabric is moderately easy to cut and sew, but pins and needles may leave holes. Choose close-fitting, fitted or semi-fitted styles to make petticoats, dresses, evening wear, bridal wear and linings. Some versions can be gently laundered at home, but drycleaning is usually recommended because taffeta is extremely difficult to iron.

Silk's scroop

In the classic story, "Gone With the Wind," Rhett Butler knows Mamie is wearing his gift, a red silk taffeta petticoat, because he hears it rustle. The rustle, called scroop, is characteristic of silk taffeta. One way to test the quality of silk taffeta is to scrunch the fabric in your hand and listen. Good taffeta will let off a distinctive rustle. If your silk petticoat is too noisy, give it a bath in warm, soapy water. To reverse the process, soak it in a solution of 5 percent white vinegar and water.

antique taffeta
A stiff-finished fabric made to resemble fabrics of the 18th century, usually made of douppioni silk or synthetic fibers.

chameleon taffeta
An iridescent taffeta made with two colors in the filling and a third color in the warp.

chiffon taffeta
A soft, glossy, lightweight taffeta.

faille taffeta
Taffeta with a pronounced crosswise rib.

moiré taffeta
Taffeta with a moiré finish.

paper taffeta
Lightweight, with a crisp, paper-like finish.

pigmented taffeta
Dull fabric made with pigment-dyed yarns.

tissue taffeta
A transparent, very lightweight taffeta.

Sewing rating
- ☐ Easy to sew
- ☒ Moderately easy
- ☐ Average
- ☐ Moderately difficult
- ☐ Extremely difficult

Suggested fit
- ☐ Stretch to fit
- ☐ Close-fitting
- ☒ Fitted
- ☒ Semi-fitted
- ☒ Loose-fitting
- ☐ Very loose-fitting

Suggested styles
- ☒ Pleats ☒ Tucks
  - ☒ pressed
  - ☐ unpressed
- ☒ Gathers
  - ☐ limp ☐ soft
  - ☐ full ☒ lofty
  - ☐ bouffant
- ☐ Elasticized shirring
- ☐ Smocked
- ☐ Tailored
- ☐ Shaped with seams to eliminate bulk
- ☐ Lined
- ☐ Unlined
- ☒ Puffed or bouffant
- ☐ Loose and full
- ☐ Soft and flowing
- ☐ Draped
- ☐ Cut on bias
- ☐ Stretch styling

What to expect
- ☐ Fabric is slippery, difficult to control
- ☒ It is easy to cut out
- ☐ Difficult to cut out
- ☐ Fabric has a nap
- ☒ Fabric is reversible
- ☒ Both sides of fabric look the same
- ☐ It stretches easily
- ☒ It will not stretch
- ☒ It is difficult to ease sleeves and curves
- ☒ Fabric tears easily
- ☐ It is difficult to tear
- ☐ Fabric will not tear
- ☒ Pins and needles leave holes, marks
- ☐ It tends to pucker
- ☐ It tends to unravel
- ☒ Fabric won't unravel
- ☐ Inner construction shows from outside
- ☐ Machine eats fabric
- ☐ Skipped stitches
- ☐ Layers feed unevenly
- ☒ It creases easily
- ☐ Won't hold a crease

Cost per yard
- ☐ Less than $10
- ☒ $10 to $20
- ☒ $20 to $30
- ☒ $30 to $40
- ☒ $40 to $50
- ☐ More than $50

Moiré pattern
Taffeta is often given a moiré finish by passing the fabric through engraved rollers and applying steam, pressure and/or chemicals. The finished fabric has a wavy or rippled pattern that resembles a water stain or mark, with dull and lustrous areas that reflect light differently. Moiré, which is French for "watered," was originally applied to lustrous fabrics of gold, silver and silk as early as the 15th century. Today, it is used on a variety of fabrics and fibers. It is usually permanent on synthetics, but washes out of silks and rayons.

Wearability
- ☒ Durable ☐ Fragile
- ☒ Strong ☐ Weak
- ☒ It is long-wearing
- ☒ It wears evenly
- ☐ It wears out along seams and folds
- ☐ Seams don't hold up under stress
- ☐ Fabric is subject to abrasion
- ☒ It resists abrasion
- ☐ Subject to snags
- ☒ It resists snags
- ☐ Subject to runs
- ☐ It tends to pill
- ☐ It tends to shed
- ☐ It attracts lint
- ☐ It attracts static
- ☐ It is static-free
- ☐ It tends to cling
- ☒ It holds its shape
- ☐ It loses its shape
- ☐ It stretches out of shape easily
- ☐ It droops, bags
- ☒ It tends to wrinkle
- ☐ It resists wrinkles
- ☐ It crushes easily
- ☒ Water drops leave spots or marks

Suggested care
- ☐ Dryclean only
- ☐ Do not dryclean
- ☒ Dryclean or wash
- ☒ Gently handwash in lukewarm water
- ☒ Roll in a towel to remove moisture
- ☐ Drip dry
- ☐ Lay flat to dry
- ☐ Machine wash
  - ☐ gentle/delicate
  - ☐ regular/normal
  - ☐ do not spin
- ☐ Machine dry
  - ☐ cool ☐ normal
  - ☐ perm. press
- ☒ Press damp fabric
- ☐ Press dry fabric
- ☒ Dry iron ☐ Steam
- ☐ Iron on wrong side
- ☐ Use a press cloth
- ☐ Use a needleboard
- ☐ Needs no ironing
- ☐ Do not iron
- ☒ Fabric may shrink
- ☒ May bleed or fade

Where to find
- ☐ Any fabric store
- ☐ Major chain store
- ☒ Stores that carry high quality fabric
- ☒ Fabric club
- ☒ Mail order
- ☒ Wholesale supplier

ATTACH SAMPLE HERE

LENGTHWISE GRAIN

Thai silk is usually lustrous and iridescent.

Thai silk

Lustrous, frequently iridescent fabrics woven by hand in Thailand, usually with a tight, balanced plain weave and ply yarns of two different colors – one for the warp and one for the filling. Fabric usually has a smooth, flat texture and a crisp, scrunchy hand with a lot of body. The weight varies from light to heavy, depending on the ply. Some versions are made with metallic yarns, increasing the shimmer and shine. When fabric is not iridescent, it is often a solid color or a bright plaid in such blinding combinations as orange and hot pink. Thai silk is occasionally printed or dyed with ikat designs.

How to use

Thai silk has a moderately crisp drape that may be pleated or gathered into a lofty fullness. The lightest weight is ideal for blouses and lingerie, the middle weight for dresses, and heavier versions tailor beautifully. Fabric ravels at the drop of a pin. Drycleaning is recommended for iridescent and plaid versions. Plain colors may be gently handwashed, but fabric may shrink, bleed or fade.

Woven by hand

Some of the most beautiful and unusual fabrics available today are made the old-fashioned way – with hand looms that require the weavers to throw shuttles by hand and lift harnesses with foot power. Hand weavers often use special yarns and a variety of weaves, adding richness and texture that can't be matched by a commercial loom. Fabrics often drape nicely and tailor well, but they also ravel easily and tend to fray and shrink. A handwoven fabric usually needs special handling and care.

four-ply silk

Heavier versions of Thai silk are made with four-ply yarns, producing a fabric called four-ply silk or four-ply crepe. This luxurious cloth is smooth and flat, with a dull luster and only a slight crepe. Fabric tailors well and drapes beautifully, but tends to ravel. Not all four-ply silks are made in Thailand.

ikat designs

Ikat is made of yarns that have been tied and dyed, rather than tying and dying the entire fabric. The blurred design looks like a reflection on water. It may be applied to the warp (warp ikat), filling (filling ikat) or both (double ikat). The dyeing technique was developed in northeastern Asia.

Korean silk

Korea, like Thailand, has a small, thriving silk industry. Fabrics are often woven by hand and can be quite luxurious, but they are produced in small quantities and are not commonly available in stores. Korea is a big producer of tussah silk; South Korea is a major source of silk for U.S. mills.

Sewing rating
- [ ] Easy to sew
- [ ] Moderately easy
- [x] Average
- [ ] Moderately difficult
- [ ] Extremely difficult

Suggested fit
- [ ] Stretch to fit
- [ ] Close-fitting
- [ ] Fitted
- [x] Semi-fitted
- [x] Loose-fitting
- [x] Very loose-fitting

Suggested styles
- [x] Pleats [x] Tucks
  - [x] pressed
  - [ ] unpressed
- [x] Gathers
  - [ ] limp [ ] soft
  - [x] full [x] lofty
  - [ ] bouffant
- [ ] Elasticized shirring
- [ ] Smocked
- [x] Tailored
- [ ] Shaped with seams to eliminate bulk
- [ ] Lined
- [ ] Unlined
- [x] Puffed or bouffant
- [x] Loose and full
- [ ] Soft and flowing
- [ ] Draped
- [ ] Cut on bias
- [ ] Stretch styling

What to expect
- [x] Fabric is slippery, difficult to control
- [ ] It is easy to cut out
- [ ] Difficult to cut out
- [ ] Fabric has a nap
- [x] Fabric is reversible
- [x] Both sides of fabric look the same
- [ ] It stretches easily
- [ ] It will not stretch
- [ ] It is difficult to ease sleeves and curves
- [x] Fabric tears easily
- [ ] It is difficult to tear
- [ ] Fabric will not tear
- [x] Pins and needles leave holes, marks
- [ ] It tends to pucker
- [x] It tends to unravel
- [ ] Fabric won't unravel
- [ ] Inner construction shows from outside
- [ ] Machine eats fabric
- [ ] Skipped stitches
- [ ] Layers feed unevenly
- [x] It creases easily
- [ ] Won't hold a crease

Cost per yard
- [ ] Less than $10
- [x] $10 to $20
- [x] $20 to $30
- [x] $30 to $40
- [ ] $40 to $50
- [ ] More than $50

Silk from Thailand

Lovers of Thai silk can thank American Jim Thompson for turning Thailand's small silk industry into a major export. Thompson visited Bangkok as a member of the National Guard and quickly fell in love with his surroundings. He collected local art, including a cloth of shimmering silk that would change his life. When his tour was up, Thompson headed north, where he found villagers using handmade bamboo looms to weave the lustrous silks. He came home with a suitcase full of Thai silks, which he quickly sold. Inspired, he formed the Jim Thompson Thai Silk Co. and returned to Bangkok to work. In 1967, he vanished mysteriously, but his shop remains.

Wearability
- [x] Durable [ ] Fragile
- [ ] Strong [ ] Weak
- [ ] It is long-wearing
- [x] It wears evenly
- [ ] It wears out along seams and folds
- [ ] Seams don't hold up under stress
- [ ] Fabric is subject to abrasion
- [ ] It resists abrasion
- [ ] Subject to snags
- [ ] It resists snags
- [ ] Subject to runs
- [ ] It tends to pill

- [ ] It tends to shed
- [ ] It attracts lint
- [ ] It attracts static
- [ ] It is static-free
- [ ] It tends to cling
- [x] It holds its shape
- [ ] It loses its shape
- [ ] It stretches out of shape easily
- [ ] It droops, bags
- [x] It tends to wrinkle
- [ ] It resists wrinkles
- [ ] It crushes easily
- [x] Water drops leave spots or marks

Suggested care
- [x] Dryclean only
- [ ] Do not dryclean
- [ ] Dryclean or wash
- [ ] Gently handwash in lukewarm water
- [ ] Roll in a towel to remove moisture
- [ ] Drip dry
- [ ] Lay flat to dry
- [ ] Machine wash
  - [ ] gentle/delicate
  - [ ] regular/normal
  - [ ] do not spin
- [ ] Machine dry
  - [ ] cool [ ] normal
  - [ ] perm. press
- [ ] Press damp fabric
- [x] Press dry fabric
- [x] Dry iron [ ] Steam
- [ ] Iron on wrong side
- [ ] Use a press cloth
- [ ] Use a needleboard
- [ ] Needs no ironing
- [ ] Do not iron
- [x] Fabric may shrink
- [x] May bleed or fade

Where to find
- [ ] Any fabric store
- [ ] Major chain store
- [x] Stores that carry high quality fabric
- [ ] Fabric club
- [x] Mail order
- [x] Wholesale supplier

Wild tussah silk is usually natural in color.

tussah silk

A medium to heavy, plain-weave fabric made with silk from uncultivated, or wild, tussah silkworms. Several fabrics are made from tussah silk, including pongee, but the classic tussah cloth has a coarse, thick hand and a rough, uneven appearance, with distinct crosswise ribs formed by irregular, slubbed filling yarns. Like most wild silks, tussah is difficult to dye, so it is usually natural in color, ranging from cream to tan to gold to brown. Fabric is sometimes bleached and/or stiffened.

Wild silk is often confused, incorrectly, with raw silk.

Most wild silk on the market is tussah, but there are others.

How to use

Tussah is a firm, stiff fabric that does not drape, pleat or gather well. It has very little give to it, making it difficult to ease sleeves and curves. It is strong, but subject to snags, abrasions and seam slippage. Crosswise yarns ravel badly. Choose fitted or semi-fitted styles with no extra bulk. Use to make suits, jackets, skirts and tailored dresses. Drycleaning is recommended.

Wild silk

Wild silk is spun by a variety of silkworms that thrive in a wild, natural environment. They eat oak, fig, plum or juniper leaves, which add various tannins to the fiber, making it darker and difficult to dye. They also spin bits of leaves and twigs into the cocoons, producing coarse, irregular fibers. Most wild silk is unreelable because the moth is allowed to emerge from the cocoon, breaking the fiber but continuing the reproductive cycle. Sometimes wild silk is cultivated, making it reelable.

Atlas silk

A gray or brown, semi-domesticated silk similar to tussah. The Atlas moth is found throughout India, especially in the south, and in Sri Lanka, Burma, China and Java. It is one of the largest silk moths, with a wingspan of up to 10 inches across. Also called Ailanthus silk and Fagara silk.

eria silk

A strong, white, wild silk from East India, Assam and Pakistan, similar to tussah.

muga silk

This fawn or gold-colored wild silk is one of the best. From India, cultivated chiefly in Assam. Also spelled moonga or mounga.

yama-mai silk

A fine, wild silk native to Japan, once used exclusively by Japanese royalty. It looks more like cultivated silk than any other wild silk, although it is coarser. The silkworm eats oak leaves and produces an unusually large, regular, green cocoon that can be easily unreeled into long filaments.

Sewing rating
- [ ] Easy to sew
- [x] Moderately easy
- [ ] Average
- [ ] Moderately difficult
- [ ] Extremely difficult

Suggested fit
- [ ] Stretch to fit
- [ ] Close-fitting
- [x] Fitted
- [x] Semi-fitted
- [ ] Loose-fitting
- [ ] Very loose-fitting

Suggested styles
- [ ] Pleats [ ] Tucks
  - [ ] pressed
  - [ ] unpressed
- [ ] Gathers
  - [ ] limp [ ] soft
  - [ ] full [ ] lofty
  - [ ] bouffant
- [ ] Elasticized shirring
- [ ] Smocked
- [x] Tailored
- [x] Shaped with seams to eliminate bulk
- [x] Lined
- [ ] Unlined
- [ ] Puffed or bouffant
- [ ] Loose and full
- [ ] Soft and flowing
- [ ] Draped
- [ ] Cut on bias
- [ ] Stretch styling

What to expect
- [ ] Fabric is slippery, difficult to control
- [x] It is easy to cut out
- [ ] Difficult to cut out
- [ ] Fabric has a nap
- [x] Fabric is reversible
- [x] Both sides of fabric look the same
- [ ] It stretches easily
- [x] It will not stretch
- [x] It is difficult to ease sleeves and curves
- [ ] Fabric tears easily
- [ ] It is difficult to tear
- [x] Fabric will not tear
- [ ] Pins and needles leave holes, marks
- [ ] It tends to pucker
- [x] It tends to unravel
- [ ] Fabric won't unravel
- [ ] Inner construction shows from outside
- [ ] Machine eats fabric
- [ ] Skipped stitches
- [ ] Layers feed unevenly
- [ ] It creases easily
- [x] Won't hold a crease

Cost per yard
- [ ] Less than $10
- [x] $10 to $20
- [x] $20 to $30
- [ ] $30 to $40
- [ ] $40 to $50
- [ ] More than $50

Tussah moths
The Chinese tussah is the best known and most abundant wild silk moth. This native of Manchuria and China eats oak leaves. The color and quality of the silk are affected by the climate and soil — Manchurian tussah is heavier and darker than tussah from the warmer region of Shantung. The Indian tussah, a close relative, flourishes all over India on a diet of jujube leaves. The worm spins a very large, reelable cocoon, but it is rarely reeled. Like most wild silks, the cocoon is usually pulled apart, carded and spun into yarn.

Wearability
- [ ] Durable [ ] Fragile
- [x] Strong [ ] Weak
- [ ] It is long-wearing
- [ ] It wears evenly
- [ ] It wears out along seams and folds
- [x] Seams don't hold up under stress
- [x] Fabric is subject to abrasion
- [ ] It resists abrasion
- [x] Subject to snags
- [ ] It resists snags
- [ ] Subject to runs
- [ ] It tends to pill
- [ ] It tends to shed
- [ ] It attracts lint
- [ ] It attracts static
- [ ] It is static-free
- [ ] It tends to cling
- [x] It holds its shape
- [ ] It loses its shape
- [ ] It stretches out of shape easily
- [ ] It droops, bags
- [ ] It tends to wrinkle
- [x] It resists wrinkles
- [ ] It crushes easily
- [ ] Water drops leave spots or marks

Suggested care
- [x] Dryclean only
- [ ] Do not dryclean
- [ ] Dryclean or wash
- [ ] Gently handwash in lukewarm water
- [ ] Roll in a towel to remove moisture
- [ ] Drip dry
- [ ] Lay flat to dry
- [ ] Machine wash
  - [ ] gentle/delicate
  - [ ] regular/normal
  - [ ] do not spin
- [ ] Machine dry
  - [ ] cool [ ] normal
  - [ ] perm. press
- [ ] Press damp fabric
- [x] Press dry fabric
- [ ] Dry iron [x] Steam
- [ ] Iron on wrong side
- [x] Use a press cloth
- [ ] Use a needleboard
- [ ] Needs no ironing
- [ ] Do not iron
- [x] Fabric may shrink
- [ ] May bleed or fade

Where to find
- [ ] Any fabric store
- [ ] Major chain store
- [x] Stores that carry high quality fabric
- [ ] Fabric club
- [x] Mail order
- [x] Wholesale supplier

ATTACH SAMPLE HERE

LENGTHWISE GRAIN

Silk tweed has colorful yarns and slubs.

tweed

A rough, nubby fabric made with slubbed, textured, thick-and-thin or novelty yarns to resemble wool tweed. It is usually a plain or twill weave, but may also be a basket weave, herringbone or novelty weave. Silk tweed may be firmly or loosely woven, but it feels rough and has a coarse appearance, with colorful, sometimes lustrous, slubs. The fabric itself is usually dull, made with a blend of spun silk and silk filament, or a blend of silk and other fibers. Filament yarns provide luster. Synthetics may be added for increased strength and durability.

How to use

Silk tweed tailors nicely, but does not pleat or gather well. The medium-light to medium-heavy fabric has a moderately stiff drape that holds the shape of the garment — it works best with fitted or semi-fitted styles that do not have a lot of bulk. Fabric resists wrinkles, but loose weaves tend to snag and unravel. Use to make suits, jackets, skirts and tailored dresses. Drycleaning is recommended, especially if the garment has lots of inner construction.

Bannockburn tweed
Originally made in Bannockburn, Scotland, by alternating single and double-ply yarns.

Donegal tweed
A thick, warm homespun with thick, colored slubs, originally of wool and handwoven by peasants in Donegal County, Ireland.

Harris tweed
Trade name for an expensive, virgin wool tweed from Harris and the other Outer Hebrides Islands off the coast of Scotland. This rough, heavy, handwoven fabric often smells like peat, especially if it gets wet. Used to make tailored coats and suits. If it isn't properly labeled, it isn't authentic.

Irish tweed
Tweed from Ireland, usually made with a twill weave, a white warp and a dark filling.

Linton tweed
Trade name for fine fabrics made by Linton Tweeds, Ltd., of Carlisle, England. Usually very soft, made from merino wool.

Sewing rating
- ☐ Easy to sew
- ☒ Moderately easy
- ☐ Average
- ☐ Moderately difficult
- ☐ Extremely difficult

Suggested fit
- ☐ Stretch to fit
- ☐ Close-fitting
- ☒ Fitted
- ☒ Semi-fitted
- ☐ Loose-fitting
- ☐ Very loose-fitting

Suggested styles
- ☐ Pleats ☐ Tucks
  - ☐ pressed
  - ☐ unpressed
- ☐ Gathers
  - ☐ limp ☐ soft
  - ☐ full ☐ lofty
  - ☐ bouffant
- ☐ Elasticized shirring
- ☐ Smocked
- ☒ Tailored
- ☒ Shaped with seams to eliminate bulk
- ☒ Lined
- ☐ Unlined
- ☐ Puffed or bouffant
- ☐ Loose and full
- ☐ Soft and flowing
- ☐ Draped
- ☐ Cut on bias
- ☐ Stretch styling

What to expect
- ☐ Fabric is slippery, difficult to control
- ☒ It is easy to cut out
- ☐ Difficult to cut out
- ☐ Fabric has a nap
- ☐ Fabric is reversible
- ☐ Both sides of fabric look the same
- ☐ It stretches easily
- ☐ It will not stretch
- ☒ It is difficult to ease sleeves and curves
- ☐ Fabric tears easily
- ☐ It is difficult to tear
- ☒ Fabric will not tear
- ☐ Pins and needles leave holes, marks
- ☐ It tends to pucker
- ☒ It tends to unravel
- ☐ Fabric won't unravel
- ☐ Inner construction shows from outside
- ☐ Machine eats fabric
- ☐ Skipped stitches
- ☐ Layers feed unevenly
- ☐ It creases easily
- ☒ Won't hold a crease

Cost per yard
- ☐ Less than $10
- ☒ $10 to $20
- ☒ $20 to $30
- ☒ $30 to $40
- ☐ $40 to $50
- ☐ More than $50

Silk blends
Silk tweed is often made with a mixture of silk and other fibers, including rayon, wool, cotton, linen and/or synthetics. One reason is to reduce the cost of the fabric while maintaining silk's allure. But not all blends are based on cost. A good marriage of different fibers can produce fabric with more desirable characteristics than either could provide alone. Silk, for example, adds warmth and breathability to synthetics, while synthetics contribute strength and abrasion resistance, especially to spun silk. Blends are made by spinning different fibers together into yarn. Some versions, more accurately called union fabrics, mix yarns of different fibers into the weave.

Wearability
- ☐ Durable ☐ Fragile
- ☐ Strong ☐ Weak
- ☒ It is long-wearing
- ☐ It wears evenly
- ☐ It wears out along seams and folds
- ☐ Seams don't hold up under stress
- ☒ Fabric is subject to abrasion
- ☐ It resists abrasion
- ☒ Subject to snags
- ☐ It resists snags
- ☐ Subject to runs
- ☒ It tends to pill

- ☐ It tends to shed
- ☐ It attracts lint
- ☐ It attracts static
- ☐ It is static-free
- ☐ It tends to cling
- ☒ It holds its shape
- ☐ It loses its shape
- ☐ It stretches out of shape easily
- ☐ It droops, bags
- ☐ It tends to wrinkle
- ☒ It resists wrinkles
- ☐ It crushes easily
- ☐ Water drops leave spots or marks

Suggested care
- ☒ Dryclean only
- ☐ Do not dryclean
- ☐ Dryclean or wash
- ☐ Gently handwash in lukewarm water
- ☐ Roll in a towel to remove moisture
- ☐ Drip dry
- ☐ Lay flat to dry
- ☐ Machine wash
  - ☐ gentle/delicate
  - ☐ regular/normal
  - ☐ do not spin
- ☐ Machine dry
  - ☐ cool ☐ normal
  - ☐ perm. press
- ☐ Press damp fabric
- ☒ Press dry fabric
- ☐ Dry iron ☒ Steam
- ☒ Iron on wrong side
- ☒ Use a press cloth
- ☐ Use a needleboard
- ☐ Needs no ironing
- ☐ Do not iron
- ☐ Fabric may shrink
- ☐ May bleed or fade

Where to find
- ☐ Any fabric store
- ☒ Major chain store
- ☒ Stores that carry high quality fabric
- ☒ Fabric club
- ☒ Mail order
- ☒ Wholesale supplier

ATTACH SAMPLE HERE

LENGTHWISE GRAIN

This velvet has silk pile and a rayon back.

velvet

Silk velvet is a true luxury fabric. It is very soft, elegant and more flattering to wear than other velvets. Fabric has a soft, limp hand and a very fragile pile that crushes easily. It looks and feels expensive, so its high price should come as no surprise. Most versions have a silk pile of low-twist filament yarns woven into a backing of another fiber, usually rayon. The most readily available silk velvet is 18% silk and 82% rayon. All-silk velvet is the most exquisite (and most costly), but it is almost impossible to find. Rayon is more common.

How to use

Silk velvet has a soft, graceful drape that falls close to the body. It may be gathered or shirred into a limp fullness. This slippery, napped fabric stretches easily and is extremely difficult to cut and sew . Choose simple styles with few seams to avoid overworking the fabric and crushing the pile. Press lightly, using steam, on a needle board with the pile against the needles. Use to make evening clothes and special occasion dresses. Dryclean only.

Velveteen

Velveteen, the cotton cousin of velvet, has a short, close pile made from soft, long-staple, combed cotton that is cut to resemble velvet. It is frequently confused with cotton velvet, but the fabrics are different. True velvet is made with a warp pile, while velveteen has a filling pile. Until World War II, velvet was usually made from silk. During the war, the source of raw silk was cut off, so cotton was used in its place, resulting in a true "cotton velvet" that is still made today.

---

brocaded velvet

A patterned velvet that resembles cut velvet, made by removing parts of the pile. Also called voided velvet.

chiffon velvet

Very lightweight fabric that drapes well. Durable, but pile crushes easily.

crushed velvet

Pile is pressed in different directions to create a pattern that changes color when fabric is moved or angle of view changes.

cut velvet

A distinct pile pattern, woven on a sheer or heavy background, with a jacquard loom.

Lyons velvet

A heavy, crisp velvet with a stiff drape. Has silk pile and cotton or rayon back, made in Lyon, France. There are many imitations.

panné velvet

Very soft and lustrous, with pile flattened in one direction. May be silk or synthetic.

Sewing rating
- [ ] Easy to sew
- [ ] Moderately easy
- [ ] Average
- [ ] Moderately difficult
- [x] Extremely difficult

Suggested fit
- [ ] Stretch to fit
- [ ] Close-fitting
- [x] Fitted
- [x] Semi-fitted
- [x] Loose-fitting
- [ ] Very loose-fitting

Suggested styles
- [ ] Pleats [x] Tucks
  - [ ] pressed
  - [x] unpressed
- [x] Gathers
  - [ ] limp [x] soft
  - [x] full [ ] lofty
  - [ ] bouffant
- [x] Elasticized shirring
- [ ] Smocked
- [ ] Tailored
- [ ] Shaped with seams to eliminate bulk
- [x] Lined
- [ ] Unlined
- [ ] Puffed or bouffant
- [x] Loose and full
- [x] Soft and flowing
- [x] Draped
- [ ] Cut on bias
- [ ] Stretch styling

What to expect
- [x] Fabric is slippery, difficult to control
- [ ] It is easy to cut out
- [x] Difficult to cut out
- [x] Fabric has a nap
- [ ] Fabric is reversible
- [ ] Both sides of fabric look the same
- [x] It stretches easily
- [ ] It will not stretch
- [ ] It is difficult to ease sleeves and curves
- [ ] Fabric tears easily
- [ ] It is difficult to tear
- [x] Fabric will not tear
- [x] Pins and needles leave holes, marks
- [ ] It tends to pucker
- [ ] It tends to unravel
- [ ] Fabric won't unravel
- [ ] Inner construction shows from outside
- [ ] Machine eats fabric
- [ ] Skipped stitches
- [x] Layers feed unevenly
- [ ] It creases easily
- [ ] Won't hold a crease

Cost per yard
- [ ] Less than $10
- [ ] $10 to $20
- [x] $20 to $30
- [x] $30 to $40
- [x] $40 to $50
- [x] More than $50

Pile fabrics
Three-dimensional pile fabrics are made by interlacing an extra set of yarns into a plain or twill background fabric. The extra yarns, or pile, form raised loops that expand to give the fabric a fluffy, fuzzy or furry surface, depending on the size of the extra yarns, the amount of twist and the type of background weave. Tightly twisted yarns tend to hold their twist, while loosely twisted yarns unwind and spread out. The pile may be short or long, and the loops may be cut or uncut. Fake fur, corduroy, velvet and terry cloth are all pile fabrics.

Wearability
- [ ] Durable [x] Fragile
- [ ] Strong [ ] Weak
- [ ] It is long-wearing
- [ ] It wears evenly
- [ ] It wears out along seams and folds
- [ ] Seams don't hold up under stress
- [x] Fabric is subject to abrasion
- [ ] It resists abrasion
- [ ] Subject to snags
- [ ] It resists snags
- [ ] Subject to runs
- [ ] It tends to pill
- [x] It tends to shed
- [x] It attracts lint
- [ ] It attracts static
- [ ] It is static-free
- [ ] It tends to cling
- [ ] It holds its shape
- [ ] It loses its shape
- [x] It stretches out of shape easily
- [ ] It droops, bags
- [ ] It tends to wrinkle
- [ ] It resists wrinkles
- [x] It crushes easily
- [x] Water drops leave spots or marks

Suggested care
- [x] Dryclean only
- [ ] Do not dryclean
- [ ] Dryclean or wash
- [ ] Gently handwash in lukewarm water
- [ ] Roll in a towel to remove moisture
- [ ] Drip dry
- [ ] Lay flat to dry
- [ ] Machine wash
  - [ ] gentle/delicate
  - [ ] regular/normal
  - [ ] do not spin
- [ ] Machine dry
  - [ ] cool [ ] normal
  - [ ] perm. press
- [ ] Press damp fabric
- [x] Press dry fabric
- [ ] Dry iron [x] Steam
- [x] Iron on wrong side
- [ ] Use a press cloth
- [x] Use a needleboard
- [ ] Needs no ironing
- [ ] Do not iron
- [ ] Fabric may shrink
- [ ] May bleed or fade

Where to find
- [ ] Any fabric store
- [ ] Major chain store
- [x] Stores that carry high quality fabric
- [ ] Fabric club
- [x] Mail order
- [x] Wholesale supplier

Start a personal swatch collection

Here's a place to collect samples of other fabrics. Some suggestions:

Look for light and heavy versions of charmeuse, chiffon, China silk and habutai. Add sheer douppioni, tissue faille, triple georgette, four-ply crepe and paper taffeta.

Look for variations of jacquard, such as noil or gazar with jacquard figures. Find iridescent versions of shantung, taffeta and organza.

Try to find samples of bengaline, gauze, gazar, illusion, ottoman and sari silk. Look for unusual silks, such as silk seersucker, corduroy with silk pile and stretch silk with Lycra®.

Collect fabrics from around the world. Find Italian prints, Liberty of London silks and Indian matka. Add different kinds of wild silk. Try to find muga silk, eria silk and yama-mai.

Or, use this space to keep track of your silk sewing projects. Record such information as the date, the fabric's price, the type of garment and the pattern number. Explain any problems you may have had with the fabric and how you solved them.

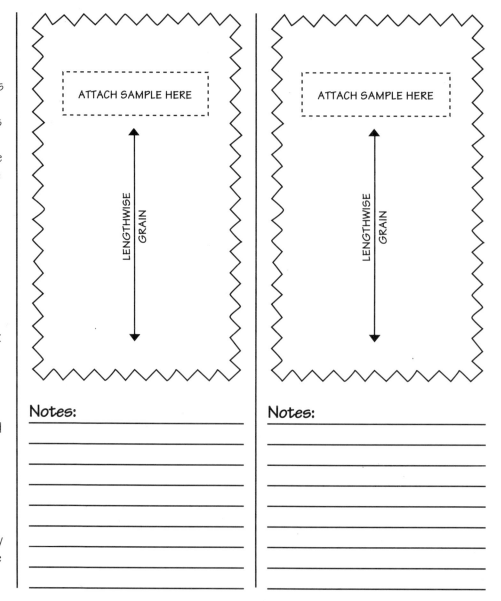

ATTACH SAMPLE HERE

LENGTHWISE GRAIN

ATTACH SAMPLE HERE

LENGTHWISE GRAIN

Notes:

_____

_____

_____

_____

_____

_____

_____

Notes:

_____

_____

_____

_____

_____

_____

_____

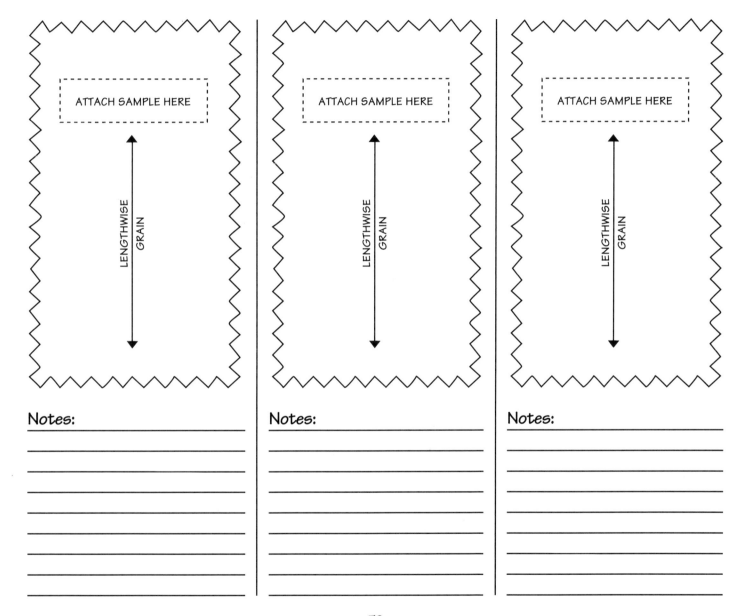

ATTACH SAMPLE HERE

LENGTHWISE GRAIN

ATTACH SAMPLE HERE

LENGTHWISE GRAIN

ATTACH SAMPLE HERE

LENGTHWISE GRAIN

Notes:

_____
_____
_____
_____
_____
_____
_____
_____

Notes:

_____
_____
_____
_____
_____
_____
_____
_____

Notes:

_____
_____
_____
_____
_____
_____
_____
_____

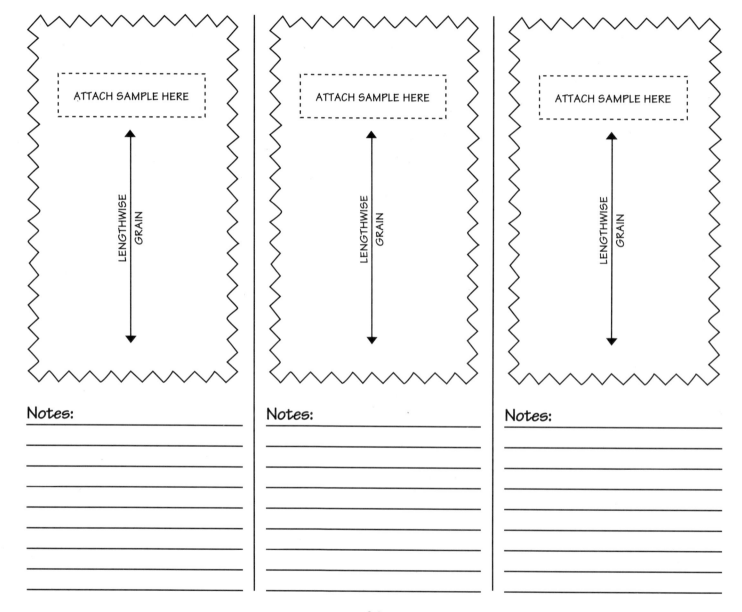

ATTACH SAMPLE HERE

LENGTHWISE GRAIN

Notes:

ATTACH SAMPLE HERE

LENGTHWISE GRAIN

Notes:

ATTACH SAMPLE HERE

LENGTHWISE GRAIN

Notes:

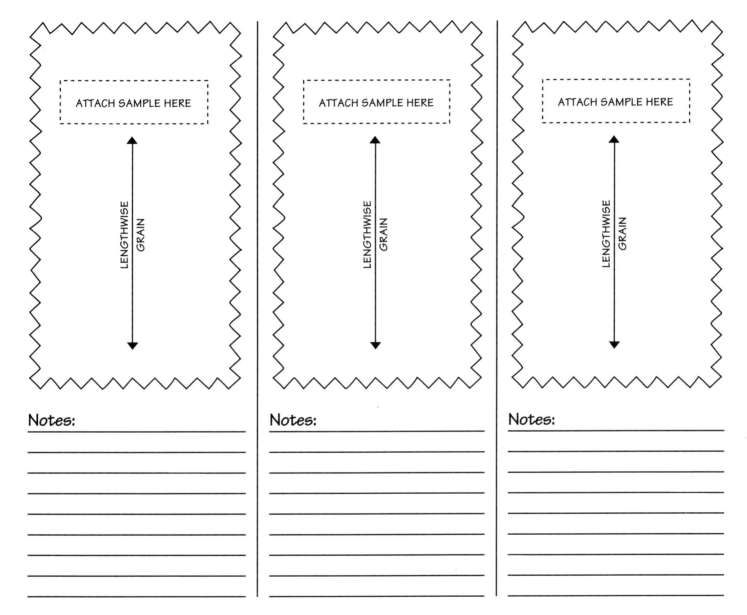

ATTACH SAMPLE HERE

LENGTHWISE GRAIN

ATTACH SAMPLE HERE

LENGTHWISE GRAIN

ATTACH SAMPLE HERE

LENGTHWISE GRAIN

Notes:

Notes:

Notes:

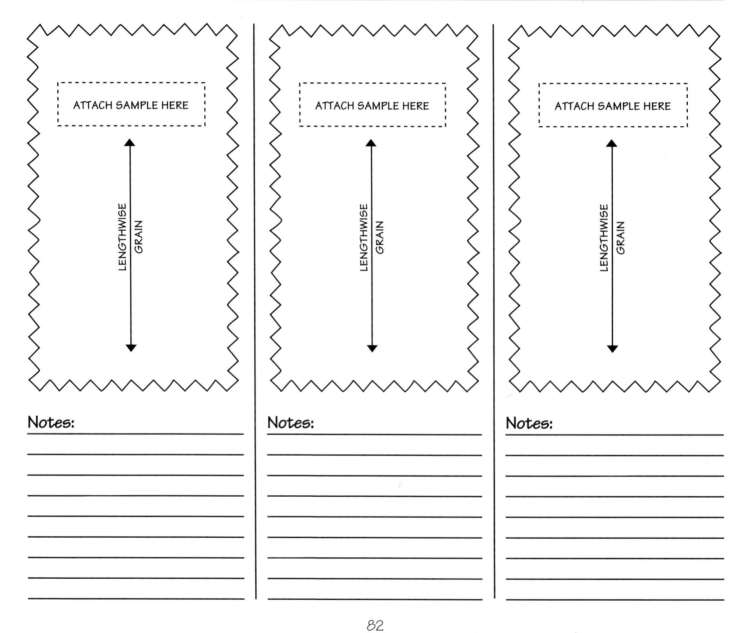

ATTACH SAMPLE HERE

LENGTHWISE GRAIN

ATTACH SAMPLE HERE

LENGTHWISE GRAIN

ATTACH SAMPLE HERE

LENGTHWISE GRAIN

Notes:

_____

_____

_____

_____

_____

_____

_____

Notes:

_____

_____

_____

_____

_____

_____

_____

Notes:

_____

_____

_____

_____

_____

_____

_____

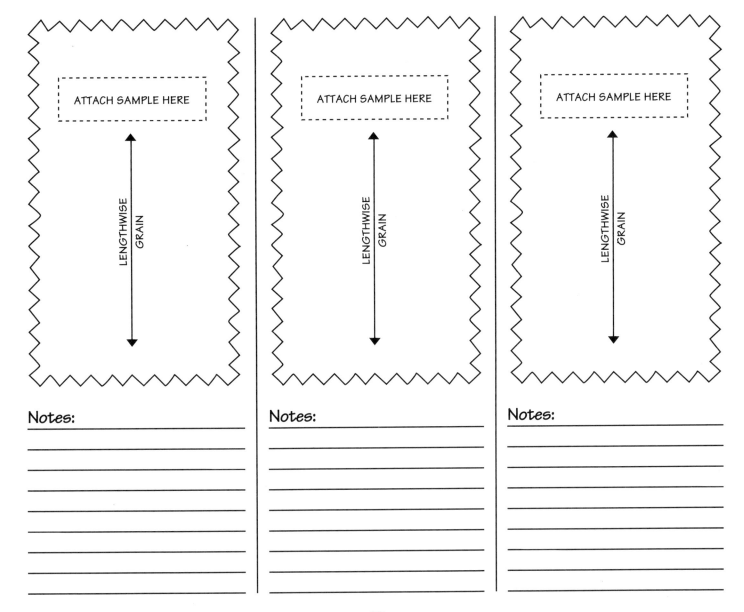

ATTACH SAMPLE HERE

LENGTHWISE GRAIN

ATTACH SAMPLE HERE

LENGTHWISE GRAIN

ATTACH SAMPLE HERE

LENGTHWISE GRAIN

Notes:

_____

_____

_____

_____

_____

_____

_____

_____

Notes:

_____

_____

_____

_____

_____

_____

_____

_____

Notes:

_____

_____

_____

_____

_____

_____

_____

_____

SHOPPING FOR SILK

It pays to shop around. If you live in an area that has several fabric stores, visit all of them. You will probably discover that each store carries some, but not all, of the silk fabrics in this book, and that prices vary.

I shop at more than 10 fabric stores, and have discovered that one store specializes in white silks, another has the most fashionable silks in all the latest colors and a third carries a wide selection of silk tweeds, but nothing else.

One of my favorite stores buys designer leftovers – it often has unusual, one-of-a-kind silk fabrics. Another store has the biggest selection with more than 300 bolts of silk fabrics, but it also has the highest prices.

If the fabric store in your area doesn't carry much silk, you may want to explore mail-order sources. This is a good way to locate unusual or hard-to-find silk fabrics, although it is difficult to accurately judge a fabric's weight, hand, drape and overall appearance by inspecting a small sample.

There are three types of sources: fabric clubs, mail-order companies and swatching services. Some are spinoffs of fabric stores, while others are mail-order specialists. Many of these sources advertise in the major sewing magazines.

Fabric clubs: Fabric clubs charge an annual fee ranging from $10 to $50 or more. Members order fabrics from catalogs and swatches that arrive in the mail at regular intervals. Most fabric clubs offer only a few silks in each mailing.

Mail-order companies: The customer pays a deposit to receive a set of fabric samples in the mail. The deposit is usually refunded when the samples are returned or if the customer places an order. Some mail-order companies specialize in silk; others carry all kinds of fabrics.

Swatching services: The store or company sends a small selection of fabric samples, based on the customer's description of the fabric she seeks. This service is sometimes free and sometimes not. Some fabric clubs provide free swatching services to their members.

Sources of silk

Baltazor Fabrics, 3406 Hessmer Avenue Metairie, LA 70002
Delicate silk fabrics, laces and supplies for bridal wear, formal occasions and fine hand sewing. Catalog available for small fee. Toll-free: 800-523-5223. Phone: 504-889-0333. E-mail: baltazor@baltazor.com. Web site: www.baltazor.com.

Britex Fabrics, 146 Geary Street San Francisco, CA 94108
Four-floor retail store with floor-to-ceiling displays of fabric of all fibers. Small fee for custom sampling to mail-order customers who provide very specific details about the types of fabrics they seek. Send a long, self-addressed stamped envelope for more information. Phone: 415-392-2910. E-mail: info@britexfabrics.com. Web site: www.britexfabrics.com.

Dharma Trading Co. 1209 Third Street, San Rafael, CA 94901
Ready-to-dye fabrics, clothing blanks and supplies for textile artists, including a nice selection of white silk fabrics, scarves and ties for dyeing or painting. Free catalog is informative and fun to read. The service is friendly and fast. Toll-free: 800-542-5227. Phone: 415-456-7657. Web site: www.dharmatrading.com.

Exotic Silks 1959 Leghorn, Mountain View, CA 94043
Wholesale source of silk fabrics from China, India and Thailand. Extensive inventory, 15-17 yard minimums. Qualified buyers only.

Phone: 650-965-7760. Toll-free (within California): 800-345-7455. Toll-free (out-of-state): 800-845-7455. Web site: www.exoticsilks.com.

Exquisite Fabrics
1775 K Street NW
Washington, D.C. 20006
Fine fabrics of all fibers imported from France, Switzerland and Italy, including couture silks, bridal fabrics and laces. Custom sampling is free to customers who send very specific details about the type of fabric they seek, including color, weight, garment style and yardage needed. Phone: 202-775-1818.

Fabric Complements
327 Central Park West
New York, NY 10025
Extensive collection of high quality fabrics of all fibers, including beautiful silk prints, three-ply and four-ply crepes, charmeuse, matka, suiting and novelties. Annual fee for seasonal mailings is higher than most fabric clubs, but you get what you pay for. Large samples are mounted on individual cards with suggestions for coordinating fabrics, garments, styles and methods of care. Phone: 212-422-4992. Web site: www.fabriccomplements.com.

Fabric Depot, 700 SE 122nd Avenue
Portland, OR 97233
Large, warehouse-style store featuring fabrics of all fibers, including the most common silks, such as charmeuse, China silk, crepe de Chine, douppioni and matka.

Discounts available on full bolts. Also handles mail orders and special requests. Toll-free: 800-392-3376. Phone: 503-252-7960. Web site: www.fabricdepot.com.

Fabrics Unlimited
5015 Columbia Pike, Arlington, VA 22204
Domestic and imported fabrics of all fibers from designer cutting rooms. Phone: 703-671-0324. Web site: www.fabricsunltd.com.

G Street Fabrics, 11854 Rockville Pike
Rockville, MD 20852
Extensive collection of fabrics of all fibers. G Street has discontinued its monthly Portfolio mailings in favor of a web site. Custom sampling is free – be specific about type of fabric, fiber, fabric weight, color, garment style, price range and yardage requirements. Also sells patterns, notions and lots of books. Has two retail

---

Updated source list
This source list was updated for our sixth printing in October 2000. For the most current list, visit our web site at www.raincitypublishing.com. Click on "Mail-order sources," then "mail-order silks."

---

stores in Virginia. Toll-free: 800-333-9191. Phone: 301-231-8960. Web site: www.gstreetfabrics.com.

Josephine's Dry Goods
521 SW 11th, Portland, OR 97205
Better quality fabrics from natural fibers, including an extensive selection of silks. Phone: 503-224-4202.

King's Road Imports
548 S. Los Angeles Street
Los Angeles, CA 90013
Wholesale source of silk fabrics from India, including matka, tweed, suiting, shantung and novelties. Qualified buyers only, low minimums. Phone: 213-624-9451. Toll-free: 800-433-1546.

Mill End Store
9701 SE McLoughlin Boulevard
Portland, OR 97222
Extensive selection of fashion fabrics of all fibers, plus home-decorating fabrics and upholstery. Lots of plain and fancy silks. For information about mail-order services, send a long, self-addressed stamped envelope. Phone: 503-786-1234. Web site: www.sewing.org/mill-end.

Mulberry Silk & Things
P.O. Box 150, Rocheport, MO 65279
Carries hard-to-find silk batting for quilted clothing and small quilts. Batts range in size from 20x40 inches to 60x80 inches. Also sells 100% silk continuous filament thread in a variety of colors. Phone: 573-698-2102. E-mail: mulberrysilk@juno.com. Web site: www.mulberrysilk.com.

Oriental Silk Company
8377 Beverly Boulevard
Los Angeles, CA 90048
More than 40 types of silk fabric, including brocade, chiffon, crepe de Chine, habutai, tussah, velvet and voile. Samples available for a small fee. For price list, send a long, self-addressed stamped envelope. Phone: 323-651-2323.

Rupert, Gibbon & Spider, Inc.
P.O. Box 425, Healdsburg, CA 95448
Ready-to-dye silk and other fabrics, plus silk scarf blanks and silk and cotton clothing for textile artists. Discounts for full bolts and large orders. Free catalog. Samples available for a small fee. Phone: 707-433-9577. Toll-free: 800-442-0455. Web site: www.jacquardproducts.com.

Sawyer Brook Distinctive Fabrics
P.O. Box 1800, Clinton, MA 01505-0813
Annual fee for seasonal mailings of fine domestic and imported fabrics, with an emphasis on natural fibers, including a nice selection of silks. Oversized samples are thoughtfully presented and packaged with care so you won't get them mixed up. Toll-free: 800-290-2739. Phone: 978-368-3133. Web site is a good place to check out their extensive button inventory: www.sawyerbrook.com.

Silk Road Textile Merchants
3910 N. Lamar Blvd., Austin, TX 78756
Retail store that sells mostly natural fibers. Silk inventory includes broadcloth, burnout silk, charmeuse, chiffon, douppioni, gauze, habutai, noil, organza, two-ply silks,

velvets. Swatches available. Phone: 512-302-0844. Web site: www.srfabrics.com.

Super Silk
P.O. Box 527596, Flushing, NY 11352
Selection includes chiffon, charmeuse, China silk, crepe de Chine, four-ply crepe, douppioni (solids, checks and stripes), organza, taffeta and tussah. Samples available for a small fee. Phone: 718-886-2606. Web site: www.supersilk.com.

Thai Silks
252 State Street, Los Altos, CA 94022
Extensive selection of silk fabrics, scarves and lingerie from China, India and Thailand, including variety of white silks for brides and textile artists. Set of about 400 samples available for a fee. Discounts available on large orders. Phone: 650-948-8611. Toll-free (within California): 800-221-7455. Toll-free (out-of-state): 800-722-7455. Web site: www.thaisilks.com.

Things Japanese
9805 NE 116th Street, PMB 7160
Kirkland, WA 98034
Silk filament thread for hand and machine sewing, in wide range of colors and weights. Also carries silk ribbons and dyes. Catalog, samples available. The owner, Maggie Backman, is a great source of information about all things silk. Phone: 425-821-2287. Web site: www.silkthings.com.

Utex Trading
710 9th Street, Niagara Falls, NY 14301
Wide selection of silk fabrics and scarves, including lots of white silks for brides and textile artists. Refundable deposit will get you one or more of three sample sets: colored silks, printed silks or white silks and natural colors. Also carries silk thread for sewing and embroidery and silk yarn for weaving or knitting. Discounts available to qualified buyers. Send long, self-addressed stamped envelope for free brochure and price list. Phone: 416-596-7565. Web site: www.utextrading.com.

ANOTHER RESOURCE

The Fashiondex, Inc.
153 W. 27th Street, New York, NY 10001
The Fashiondex is a resource guide for the apparel industry that is updated several times a year. The soft-cover, comb-bound book is expensive, but it contains wholesale sources of fabrics, buttons, trims, belt buckles and other findings, plus lots of information that is useful to designers and entrepreneurs. Company listings include minimum-yardage requirements, so if you're looking for 50 yards of silk crepe, you won't waste time calling companies with 2,000-yard minimums. Phone: 212-647-0051. Web site: www.fashiondex.com.

# GLOSSARY

all silk: The same as pure silk and pure-dye silk.

Anaphe silk: A wild silk produced by the Anaphe silkworm found in Africa, especially in Uganda. Similar to tussah, but requires stronger degumming methods because it contains a large amount of sericin.

bave: The natural silk thread spun by the silkworm. It contains two single filaments, called brins, which are held together by sericin, a natural silk gum.

blaze: The first silk produced by the silkworm, considered to be waste because the short fibers are heavily coated with sericin and do not take dye. Also called floss, Neri silk and wadding.

boiled-off silk: Silk that has been de-gummed by boiling the fiber to loosen the sericin.

bright silk: An industry term for boiled-off, thrown silk that has been dyed.

brin: A single filament of silk. The silkworm spins two of these strands at once. They are held together by a natural gummy agent, called sericin, to form a double strand used to make the cocoon.

Byssus silk: A silk-like fiber secreted from a variety of marine mollusks. Also called pinna silk, sea silk or mussel silk.

Canton silk: A type of silk reeled from very small cocoons in southern China. The fiber is soft and lustrous, but lighter in weight

---

ARTIFICIAL SILK

Artificial silk is an obsolete term used before 1925 in England and the United States to describe fabrics made of rayon and acetate, which were hailed as inexpensive copies of silk. The term was dropped after the Federal Trade Commission ruled that it was misleading. Other early names for rayon and acetate fabrics included art silk (short for artificial), imitation silk, colonial silk and wood silk (made from pulp). The list also includes Chardonnay silk, Besancon silk, Cellestron silk, Eagle silk, Stearn silk, Lowe silk, Elberfeld silk, Celluolo-silk, Collodion silk, Pauly silk, despaissis silk, Pyroxylin silk, Lehner silk, Fibersilk and Lustro silk.

---

and not as strong as regular silk. Average weight of a bale of silk is 135 pounds, but Canton silk bales weigh about 106 pounds.

changeable silk: Another name for shot or iridescent silk.

cultivated silk: Used to describe fabrics made of cultivated, rather than wild, silk.

degummed silk: Silk that has had the natural gum, or sericin, removed, usually by boiling the silk yarn or fabric in a soapy solution. Degummed silk is more desirable because it is softer and more lustrous.

denier: An international system for measuring and numbering filament yarns of silk and synthetic fibers. The finer the yarn, the lower the number. The term originally referred to an old French coin. Its weight was used as the unit of measure for silk.

dobby weave: A figure weave produced by an attachment on the loom that weaves an extra set of yarns into a simpler background weave. Dobby fabrics usually have small birdseye, dot or other geometric patterns.

dram: A unit of measure equal to 1/16 of an ounce, once used to measure silk in the United States and England. It has been replaced by the denier system.

dynamited silk: Slang for weighted silk.

end: An industry term for the lengthwise yarns on a loom or in a fabric.

filament: Silk fiber in its natural state. The long fibers are used in yarns that make smooth, lustrous fabrics. Filament can be cut to shorter lengths, which changes the characteristics of the yarn, and ultimately, of the fabric.

filling: The official, industry term for the crosswise yarns on a loom.

floss: Short silk fibers or waste silk that cannot be reeled.

fully degummed silk: Silk that has had all its gum removed. Some silk is only partially degummed.

gauze weave: A variation of the leno weave that interlaces pairs of warp yarns around the filling yarns in a figure 8 configuation.

glacé silk: Another name for changeable,

iridescent or shot silk.

gum silk: Silk that still has its sericin. It has not been degummed.

in the gum: Used to describe raw silk that has not been degummed.

leno weave: A type of open weave made by arranging warp yarns in pairs, and twisting them alternately in a right- or left-hand direction before inserting the filling yarn. This configuration adds strength to open weaves and prevents yarns from shifting out of position. Also called a doup weave.

matka: A handwoven fabric made in India of spun silk.

mulberry silk: Another name for cultivated silk, produced by silkworms that feed on the leaves of mulberry trees.

near-silk: An obsolete term for mercerized cotton lining fabric, now considered a misnomer.

organzine: Raw silk yarns of two or more twisted singles, which are then doubled and given a tight twist in the other direction. Usually used as the warp yarns on a loom.

pick: Another name for crosswise yarns.

purse silk: A soft silk embroidery thread.

reeled silk: Silk yarns with only a slight twist, made by winding the filament directly from several cocoons.

reeling: The process of unwinding raw silk from unbroken cocoons. The cocoons are usually placed in hot water to soften the sericin. Filaments from several cocoons are reeled together to form a single thread.

IN OTHER LANGUAGES

Here's a list of foreign words for silk:
- **Chinese:** si or sse.
- **French:** soie.
- **German:** Seide.
- **Greek:** serikon.
- **Hungarian:** selyem.
- **Italian:** seta.
- **Japanese:** kinu or sanski.
- **Korean:** sir or soi.
- **Latin:** sericum.
- **Russian:** sheolk.
- **Spanish:** seda.

---

rusty silk: A defect in white or pastel silk fabric that looks like rust.

sateen: A variation of satin, made with floats formed by filling rather than warp yarns. Sateen is usually made of cotton.

sea silk: Strong, lustrous fibers from a type of algae.

sericin: The natural silk gum that protects the fiber. When the sericin is removed, the fabric becomes much softer and more lustrous. It usually is not removed until after weaving.

sericulture: The care and feeding of the silkworm from egg to moth. Also called silk culture.

silk floss: Short fibers of waste silk.

silk goods: A fabric that appears to be made of silk, but has a filling of another fiber. Velvet made with silk pile and a

---

cotton back is an example.

silk gum: Another name for sericin.

soft silk: Silk that has been degummed.

spider silk: Silk filament spun by spiders, obtained by "milking" the female spider, making it impractical for textile use. Spider silk is used to make fine crosshairs in gunsights and other optical instruments.

staple fiber: Short fibers from damaged, unreelable cocoons. Used to make spun silk.

swivel weave: A type of loom that uses a small shuttle to weave an extra set of filling yarns into the fabric in a design that resembles embroidery. It is an expensive form of weaving, and thus, not common.

thrown silk: After raw silk is reeled, it is "thrown," meaning to group and twist into different types of yarn.

tram: Raw silk yarns that are doubled and given a loose twist. Usually used as filling.

vegetable silk: Lustrous hair fibers obtained from the seed pods of various plants and trees. Also called silk cotton.

warp: The official, industry terminology for the lengthwise yarns on a loom.

waste silk: Waste or short filaments that are spun into thick and thin yarns.

weft: Another name for crosswise yarns, although filling is the preferred term.

yarns: The textile industry's term for the individual threads on a loom or in a fabric. The term is not meant to suggest the thick yarns used for knitting sweaters.

BIBLIOGRAPHY

"A Dictionary of Textile Terms." 13th ed. New York: Dan River Inc., 1980.

Anderson, Enid. "The Spinner's Encyclopedia." Great Britain, David & Charles, 1987.

Brown, Gail. "Sensational Silk: A Handbook for Sewing Silk and Silk-like Fabrics." Portland, Oregon: Palmer/Pletsch Inc., 1987.

Corbman, Bernard P. "Textiles: Fiber to Fabric." 5th ed. New York: McGraw-Hill, Inc., 1975.

"Encyclopedia of Textiles." Englewood Cliffs, New Jersey: Prentice-Hall, Inc., 1960.

Feltwell, John. "The Story of Silk." New York: St. Martin's Press, 1990.

Gioello, Debbie Ann. "Profiling Fabrics: Properties, Performance and Construction Techniques." New York: Fairchild Publications, 1981.

_____. "Understanding Fabrics: From Fiber to Finished Cloth." New York: Fairchild Publications, 1982.

Hardingham, Martin. "The Fabric Catalog." New York: Simon & Schuster Pocket Books, 1978.

Hollen, Norma and Jane Saddler and others. "Textiles." 6th ed. New York: Macmillan, 1988.

Houck, Catherine. "The Fashion Encyclopedia." New York: St. Martin's Press, 1982.

Hyde, Nina. "The Queen of Textiles." *National Geographic.* Jan. 1984. p: 2-49.

Joseph, Marjory L. "Essentials of Textiles." 2nd ed. New York: Holt, Rinehart and Wilson, 1980.

Kolander, Cheryl. "A Silk Worker's Notebook." Loveland, Colorado: Interweave Press, Inc., 1985.

Lyle, Dorothy Siegert. "Modern Textiles." New York: John Wiley & Sons, Inc., 1976.

McRae, Bobbi A. "The Fabric and Fiber Sourcebook: Your One-and-Only Mail-Order Guide." Newtown, Connecticut: Taunton Press, Inc., 1989.

Miller, Edward. "Textiles: Properties and Behaviour in Clothing Use." London: B.T. Batsford, 1989.

"Only Silk Is Silk." Great Britain: Silk Association of Great Britain, 1986.

Pizzuto, Joseph J. "Fabric Science." 5th ed. revised by Arthur Price and Allen C. Cohen. New York: Fairchild Publications, 1987.

Ross, Mabel. "The Encyclopedia of Hand Spinning." Loveland, Colorado: Interweave Press, Inc., 1988.

Shaeffer, Claire. "Fabric Sewing Guide." Radnor, Pennsylvania: Chilton Book Company, 1989.

"Silk: How and Where It Is Produced." Macclesfield, Cheshire: H.T. Gaddum and Company, Ltd., 1989.

"Silk: Its Origin, Culture and Manufacture." Florence, Massachusetts: The Corticelli Silk Company, 1911.

"Sewing Specialty Fabrics." Minnetonka, Minnesota: Cy DeCosse Inc., 1986.

"Textile Handbook." Washington, D.C.: American Home Economics Association, 1964.

Wingate, Isabel B. "Fairchild's Dictionary of Textiles." 6th ed. New York: Fairchild Publications, 1984.

_____. "Textile Fabrics and Their Selection." 7th ed. Englewood Cliffs, New Jersey: Prentice-Hall, Inc., 1976.

NDEX

OTHER BOOKS IN THE SERIES

For more information about books in Julie Parker's **Fabric Reference Series**, write to Rain City Publishing, P.O. Box 15378, Seattle, WA 98115-0378 or call 206-527-8778 weekdays from 8 a.m. to 5 p.m. Pacific Time. If you send us a fax, we'll fax back an order form. Our fax number is 206-526-2871.

VOLUME II

All About Cotton: A Fabric Dictionary & Swatchbook

120 pages plus 40 cotton samples. Revised edition published in 1998. ISBN 0-9637612-3-4. LCCN: not yet known.

Comprehensive introduction covers characteristics of the fiber, history of cotton, types of cotton, the main sources of cotton, the cotton textile industry, caring for cotton and how to judge quality, followed by descriptions and samples of 40 cotton fabrics, in this order: batik, batiste, broadcloth, calico, canvas, chambray, chenille, chino, chintz, corduroy, damask, denim, dotted Swiss, double knit, drill, duck, eyelet, flannel, gauze, gingham, interlock, jersey, lawn, Madras, monk's cloth, muslin, organdy, osnaburg, oxford cloth, piqué, plissé, poplin, sateen, seersucker, shirting, terry cloth, ticking, twill, velveteen, voile.

All About Cotton is packed with information about the different yarns, weaves and finishing techniques used to make cotton fabrics. Terms such as combed cotton, mercerized cotton, pima cotton, thread count and sizing are clearly explained. This is the only guide you'll ever need to cotton fabrics. If you work with cotton, you simply shouldn't be without this book.

VOLUME III

All About Wool: A Fabric Dictionary & Swatchbook

144 pages plus 35 wool samples. Published in 1996. Second printing 1998. ISBN 0-9637612-2-6. LCCN 96-92209.

Comprehensive introduction covers characteristics of the fiber, history of wool, breeds of sheep, types of wool, the main sources of wool, the wool textile industry, new technology and wool quality, followed by descriptions and samples of 30 wool fabrics and five luxurious specialty hair fibers, in this order: blanket cloth, boiled wool, bouclé, cavalry twill, challis, coating, crêpe, Donegal tweed, double cloth, double knit, felt, flannel (woolen), flannel (worsted), gabardine, glen plaid, Harris tweed, herringbone, homespun, houndstooth, jacquard, jersey, loden cloth, melton, menswear suiting, novelty suiting, plaid, satin, tropical suiting, tweed, whipcord, alpaca, angora rabbit, camel's hair, cashmere, mohair.

All About Wool is packed with information about the yarns, weaves and finishing techniques used to make woolen and worsted fabrics. Terms such as virgin wool, lamb's wool, merino wool, superfine wool and reused wool are clearly explained. A special section describes similar fibers from other animals, such as camels and goats, making it the complete book of wool fibers and fabrics.

THE CRITICS ARE RAVING ABOUT ALL ABOUT SILK...

"A new concept in sewing books is not easy to come by, but Julie Parker has one and it's a winner. Her **All About Silk** includes real samples of 32 different fabrics, which clarifies in the most obvious way what a *matelassé* or a *peau de soie* actually looks and feels like. ... Great idea!"
— **David Page Coffin, Threads magazine**

"The 32 swatches give you a chance for hands-on evaluation of the various silk types before seeking one for your next silk creation. ... A readable and enjoyable exploration from the 'soft-as-down' habutai to the slubs and texture of douppioni."
— **Ann Price, Sew News magazine**

"Julie Parker has produced a wonderful guide to silk fabrics that is a joy to read and feel."
— **The Weaving Works, Seattle, Washington**

"Something about this book drew me into opening the cover, and from that point on I was hooked! This is no ordinary fabric dictionary. It is a visually beautiful book, enticing the reader with a clear layout, interesting graphics, and best of all, large beautiful fabric swatches!"
— **Vivian Poon, Costume Society of America**

"This thorough and well organized handbook will prove valuable to anyone working with silk, whether focusing on clothing design or construction."
— **Julie Berner, Northwest Fiber Network**

"Have you ever wondered whether a book is really written with you in mind? ... The problem most of us encounter with textile dictionaries is that we have no idea what they are talking about! Written for those actually working in the industrial end of textiles, these dictionaries are far too technical for the home sewer and they don't answer any of the practical questions. **All About Silk** takes a completely different approach."
— **G Street Fabrics, Rockville, Maryland**

"Unlike many textile reference books, **All About Silk** is understandable and not at all dry. The attractive layout of the book should win an award for clarity and ease of use."
— **Teri Hales, Sewer's SourceLetter**

"Waddayawanna know about silk? Here it is, and I dare you to find all this info on your own. Things you've always wanted to know but didn't even try to find out because you didn't know where to start looking."
— **Dharma Trading Co., San Rafael, California**

"At last, there are two resource books available to the home sewer that provide everything you need to know about cotton and silk. ... Easy to use and a pleasure just to leaf through, these books are definitely worthy of being included in your home library."
— **Vogue Patterns magazine**